Such a Lucky Boy

Laszlo Kadar

Strategic Book Publishing and Rights Co.

Strategic Book Publishing and Rights Co.
12620 FM 1960, Suite A4-507
Houston, TX 77065
www.sbpra.com

ISBN: 978-1-61204-582-5

Typography and page composition by J. K. Eckert & Company, Inc.

Dedicated to my parents, the only parents I knew:

Helen (Kaisler) and Ede Kádár (Kupferstein)

I want to thank my wife Marika for her patience

while I was writing this book.

Contents

Preface

My question is if G-d or successions of coincidences shape our future. I speculate that our destiny is driven by political ideologies, natural disasters, and the fight between good and evil. I never understood the truth behind my life and I suspect that most of you are in the same boat, not understanding the truth. We would probably never appreciate the meaning of life and death.

I am writing these words, which are philosophical in nature, but I am not a trained philosopher. I am a man already in his golden years, armed with life-experiences that were not necessarily different from many of my contemporaries. I look back into my life and wonder: "Why am I here?" I think it is normal reminiscing about the past and I am certain many "senior citizens" like me often do the same. When we get older, we might want to look back at our accomplishments. Let me share some of my life with you.

I came to the US in 1966 from Hungary. Why did I do this? I cannot give you a definite answer. For many years, my father dreamed of going to the "golden land" of Brooklyn where every Jew was happy and rich. We, my mother and I, helped him to realize his dream with the help of the Hungarian communist government who after 10 years of trying, finally issued a visa to Israel; but we never went there except to visit relatives.

I got married to my first wife, Julia, a year after my mother died her dream of enjoying grandchildren and her son getting married never having materialized. It was my fault, I was picky, and I found my soul mate too late. My daughter, Susan was two and a half, when my father passed away. He died before my son Daniel was born. My children were robbed of knowing my parents as their grandparents. At least they enjoyed their maternal grandparents for a while.

Not long before Daniel was born, my wife Julia got diagnosed with a brain tumor. Her operation failed to cure her. Because of her sickness, she could not take care of our children. As much as an old couple was able to do, my in-laws tried to help us to raise our children. Soon after my son was born, my mother-in-law developed breast cancer. Surgery, chemotherapy was followed and few years later, she left us forever. Three years later, my wife had a fatal accident, and she too left us forever.

I was alone with two young children and their closest relative was an elderly grandfather living four thousand miles away in Hungary. To better take care of my children, I had to find a steady job to provide food on the table and a roof over our heads. This job was in New Jersey. We did not know anybody there, but to avoid a long commute and to be able to spend more time with my children, I moved away from my friends and away from a few distant relatives. My challenges were well known among these people. However, they (conveniently) ignored us. When I confronted them, they claimed: "We do not want to bother you while you're having your problems." Sure, who wants to "bother" with someone else's problems? Probably they had their own or they did not care! I believe the latter one was true. I was hoping for a few kind words of encouragement, but those words never came. My life was miserable. The only thing that brought smiles on my face was my children. Would there be anything else, that could go wrong in my life? It sure could.

It was the summer of 1991. My children, for the last time, traveled alone to Hungary to spend their summer vacation with their grandfather. I was alone and frankly, I was bored. I was missing my children. I worked hard and had only a few friends in New Jersey.

I remembered the small leather portfolio left by my father, which contained documents like old birth and death certificates, marriage licenses of some distant, unknown relatives, and property transfer certificates saved from his job as the Director of Displaced Properties in Hungary. I started to take a closer look at these papers and mostly I found the kind documents that I expected to find. Then the "bombshell" hit me as nothing else had ever hit me. I found an old, fragile, yellowed, wrinkled, typewritten official document with official stamps and numerous signatures: an Adoption Certificate, dated April 5, 1948. *I WAS ADOPTED!* How was this possible? Could this be authentic? It had to be, it looked official.

A 9100/1947 Kor.sz, rendelet 321 -/ : / po tja alapján bélyegmentes.

Örökbefogadási szerződés.

Mely egyrészről Kádár me és neje Kaisler Helén békéscsabai II-
ker. Trefort u. 3 sz.a. lakosok örökbefogadják a békési állami születési
anyakönyvbe 1948 év január hó 9-én találtgyermekként bejegyzett kiskoru
Földvári László nevü gyermek,öt házukba és családjuk ba fo adják átveszik
felette az apai hatalmat illetve és t. gyámságot s gyakorolni fogják
mindazon jo okat,melyek a törvénynél fogva az örökbefogadó szülőket megilletik s elvállalják mindazon kötelezettségeket,melyek a törvénynél fogva
a szülőket terhelik s feljogositják őt mindazon jogokkal,melyek a törvénynél fogva a törvényes leszármazó örökösöket ezen minőségükben megilletik
s végül kötelezik őt,hogy eddigi családi nevének elhagyásával ezután a
"K á d á r" családi nevet viselje.

2. Alolirott Pintér Lajos békési IV.ker. Berlini u. 8 sz.a. lakos mint a kiskoru Földvári László részére Békésvármegye árvaszéke által
kirendelt gyám az 1-ső pontban foglaltak mellett kiskoru földvári László nevü gyámoltamat Kadár de és neje Kaisler Helén békéscsabai
lakosoknak örökbe adott s a Kádár rozódé
gadási szerzodésta kiskoru érdekében is jóváhagyólag megadja jóvás azu-
tan kormányhatósági megerősités céljából az Igazságügyminisztériumhoz fel-
ter szíveskedjék.

Jelen örökbefogadási szerződés szerződő felek előtt felolvas -
tatott,megmagyaráztatott s miután tartalmukkal mindenben egyező általuk el-
fogadva tanuk előtt aláiratott.

Békés 1948 január hó 15-én

előttünk:

örökbefogadók

örökbeadó
Békésvármegye árvaszéke által
5787/1-1948 á. számu véghatározat-
tal kirendelt gyám.

antieket ma is fatartom.
Békés 1948 i bi m 17-én

előttünk:

OFFICIAL ADOPTION CERTIFICATE OF LASZLO KADAR

How could I describe how I felt? How would you react to this shocking discovery? What would you do with this information? What should I do? Should I tell anyone? Do I want to tell it to anyone? Who were my "real" parents? Could I to find them? Do I want to find them? Did anyone know about this? Why I had never been told?

I never had any inkling about this fact. Nobody, including my close relatives, ever told me about this "minor detail" of my existence. My loving parents treated me, as any other parents would care for their own children; I was taken care of better than many others were. My whole life ran through in my mind. I was looking for clues that would give me a hint about my life I never knew. According to the adoption certificate, I had been about four years old when I was adopted. Could I remember something about this life-altering event?

Some memories came alive. Many questions ran through my mind some new and some I had asked before. I had gotten answers to some of these questions when I was a child, but now I realized these questions had never been truthful. The answers were stories of deceptions, not malicious, but the kind that would satisfy a child's curiosity.

"Dad is it interesting, that I was born on your birthday?" ("Interesting is it?" came the answer.) "Why was I born in the town Békés, my parents were living far away from this town?" ("You were actually born in Budapest, but during the war, all of your records were destroyed.") "Why was this woman holding me in her arms?" ("You know that we were taken to concentration camps by the Nazis. Before mommy was taken, she left you with this woman until we came back.") When I was a child, the last explanation triggered another question: "What was she doing in Nagydobos, my mother's hometown, during the war, far away from Békés?" I had never gotten any answers to this question. Suddenly, I remembered something that puzzled me ever since I was a child. It was a frightening dream. A dream that was haunted me for years. Was it a dream?

I am at home, maybe alone, or maybe someone else is there too. The front door of the house or apartment suddenly opens up. People come through the door, they are tall, and they are wearing long black (dark) winter coats. They grab me and take me outside. A large black automobile is parked on the street. We all get into the back seat. I am being held someone inside the car. I want to get out, but the automobile speeds away and I am taken somewhere.

My parents always assured me that this was only a dream. As a child, I accepted it. Now, after I found my Adoption Certificate, I knew this "dream" was real. What should I do with my secret? Should I tell anyone about it? Should I be ashamed? Should I be happy to have found loving parents who gave me a happy childhood? Why had they kept this from me? Later, I discovered everyone knew about my adoption but me. They been asked to never tell and they never told me until I asked them. Should I share this with my children?

By this time, I was in a relationship with my current wife Marika. She was the first person I told about my adoption. It was a relief for me to share the burden of knowledge. For a number of years the knowledge of my adoption was lingering in the background, everyday life took precedent. A few years had passed since the discovery and I wanted to know more about my adoption and searched for more clues in the leather portfolio.

I am returning now to my philosophical dissertation. I am writing these words when I am 66 years old and battling with cancer. I am still wondering about the actions of G-d. In 1945, an eight or nine month old boy was found abandoned at a railroad station in war-torn Hungarian countryside. A kind family took this child into their home and gave him love. Another family fought to take this child into their home to give him love and a Jewish identity. Why did G-d do all this for me?

My life has been full of both tragedies and happiness, but now I feel that G-d has deserted me. What was his purpose in saving me from certain demise and now why do I have to fight cancer? Was it happiness or suffering was destined for me? I have no answers to these questions. Nobody has answers to these kinds of questions.

One aspect of my life becomes crystal clear. The discovery of my adoption gave me an additional purpose in life. In May 1999, more than 10 years ago, I started to write the story of my life. I never knew I could write more than business letters and technical documents. The jury is still out. I discovered the excitement of creating something that others may enjoy. The main character of "Such a Lucky Boy" is Lacika using my Hungarian nickname. My parent's names were Ede and Helen.

I have lived through a turbulent time of the twentieth century, but I did not know this when I was a child. My parents always told me "you are such a lucky boy. (Nagyon szerencsés fiú vagy.)" I never knew why they said it, but now I understand. I am hoping that I could share my experiences, with my own generation who lived though this era. I want to educate the younger generation, so they realize how much better their life is without communism or under any r sort of tyranny. The events in this book are combination of factual events (personal and historical) mixed in with pure fiction and with fictional and real character's names. My father was a great storyteller and I am sorry that I never recorded many, many of the stories of my father when he was still alive. Some tales in this book were his stories and I tried to present them the way I remember them. I also believe some of his stories may have indeed been pure fictional stories. I loved these stories and everyone else who listened to my father enjoyed them; I hope you will, too. I had to complete this book before I forgot them all. I hope you enjoy reading this book as much as I have enjoyed writing it.

—October 2010

1

the boy

The cold wind hit his face after he left his small office in the train station. The fresh air felt good. The cold rain had finally stopped. The days are short in October around this part of Hungary and the constant heavy overcast sky almost never let the sunshine touch the earth. However, this particular evening was different. The thick clouds decided to move on and let the sun show its shining face to the people below. It was late and by this time, the sun had started its descent after its brief appearance, painting the sky a bright red. Part of the sky looked clear blue, on other parts, the grayish white clouds were still visibility painted with a touch of red opaque coat, and this strangely colored cloud has disrupted the unusually bright sky. As the sun slowly sank, rays from the sun reflected on these heavy clouds painting them bright red. This visual effect of the sun and clouds was an amazing sight, which is hard to describe in plain words. Normally rain clouds look somewhat flat, sometimes they are gray, and sometimes they are fluffy white with a touch of gray. Today the sun created an effect that made the clouds look three-dimensional and they looked like an island in the middle of the open sea. This island was covered with mountains and it appeared as if the upside-down mountain was covered with flaming fire. While the fire was burning, the dominating red color was getting darker and darker making it appear as if the fire was subsiding. This change was so quick that if you would look away for a moment you would missed the whole illusion as the sun slowly disappeared on the horizon. The colors of the clouds were slowly turning back into their natural boring grayish substance and the beautiful scenery had disappeared.

The man did not pay any attention to the scenery. By this time, he already had more than enough to drink. The bright sunshine helped him to feel a little bit better and gave him a sense that he was moving toward something better. As a typical Hungarian, János found alcohol irresistible. His favorite hard liquor was the plum brandy (Szilva Pálinka), favored by many of his contemporaries. Drinking helped him keep his sanity at least that is what he told himself and his wife. Drinking plum brandy, beer, cheap wine, whichever he could put his hand on, gave him a warm sense of coziness, and helped him forget about how insane the world had become.

It was October 1945, only a few months since World War II had officially ended. The destruction, which had occurred during the war, was still visible and would be visible for a long time. Broken families, broken lives, broken hearts… People lost their friends, lost their families, lost their loved ones because of the prejudice and greed of the "Third Reich" and its allies. In general, life had slowly started to return to normal. How can anyone call life normal after an event where millions of people perished? Life was far from good. People were reminiscing about their life before the war. They were hoping but no one truly believed that good times would ever come again.

János Hajdú was drafted by the Hungarian army in the early part of the war. Shortly after his basic training was completed, his unit was moved to somewhere in the Ukraine to fight against the Russian army. During his first battle, he was wounded and sent home. He got his disability papers from the army, which was fine with him. He, not unlike his fellow compatriots, did not want to abandon his family and fight in this senseless war. He never understood the reason for the war nor did he ever care to acknowledge its reason. After his wounds were healed, he found a job with the railroad police in Földvár and he was soon promoted to chief officer of the local railroad police. This sounds impressive, but do not be impressed; he had only one deputy who completed most of the work around the station. He was very happy with his new position because he got a pay raise and he had to work less.

A new world order had already started in Hungary. The occupying Russian soldiers were being moved around; some of them were going home to their own misery while others were coming into Hungary to replace those who left.

It was somewhat ironic, that János was wounded fighting against the same Russian army now occupying Hungary. At first, it felt strange that not long ago these Russians were his "enemies" and now the soldiers of the same Red Army were his liberators and his "friends." János and the Russians had at least one thing in common:

they would never refuse a drink as long as it had alcohol in it. He was getting plenty of vodka from the Russian soldiers, which helped him to accept this strangeness as an acceptable reality. The Russians were master drinkers who drunk vodka, the national drink of Russia. Even though vodka did not have that wonderful aroma of plum brandy, János started to get used to the taste so he was able to continue with his usual habit of not refusing any drink other than water. János never wanted to fall behind new comrades and as a result, the heavy drinking had become the highlight of the day (and many other days).

Today, like many other ordinary fall days, had started out the same as many other eventless, boring days in the near past. An unusual event was on the horizon and it will turn this day into the beginning of a life-changing event for him and for others. Certainly, these events would not change world history nor would it make significant changes in world events, nor would many people know about this. However, the future of at least one person was changed forever.

§ § § § § §

Földvár was a tiny village with a railroad station, not far from a larger town of Békés. The extension rail line passes through the village and connects Békés to the main railroad line that starts at Budapest and continues into Rumania. Trains stop here only once or twice a day; it was not a busy railroad station. Sometimes, in-transit freight cars either were parked at the station waiting for cargo or just parked there to allow other trains to get ahead on the main line.

Earlier that day, a long train from Budapest filled with Russian soldiers stopped at Földvár for several hours. The locomotive, for some reason, left for Békéscsaba, a large provincial town nearby. The soldiers were waiting for the locomotive to return, so they could continue their journey. János did not mind soldiers anymore. He had met many foreign soldiers; Germans, Rumanians, and Russians during the war and now the Russians, or rather the army of the Soviet Union, the Red Army was reappearing in his life. The Russian soldiers always respected authority and they were friendly with János. However, the Russian soldiers had a terrible reputation and this reputation was not earned without reason. The Russians considered themselves as liberators, and as an occupying force, they had absolutely no respect for the local population. Rape, murder, and taking property from the locals such watches and jewelry was the norm for the mighty Red Army. Who would dare argue with armed men out of control?

It may not be surprising to find that János had gotten along with the German soldiers just as well, if not better, than with the Russian soldiers. János never really had any reason to hate the Germans. As a Christian, none of the events of the past couple of decades seriously affected his life, except for the short time he spent on the Russian front. He had seen many of his Jewish neighbors disappear, but these people were neither his friends nor his enemies. Like many Hungarians, he did not care what happened to Jews. Many of his friends hated Jews, mostly because the lifestyle of Jews was so different from the lives of the peasants around them. Most people hated Jews for reasons that were not clearly defined in their minds. The old misconception that the Jews had killed Christ was taught by the church to their faithful peasants for centuries. These teachings kept alive the hatred against Jews. Many politicians seeking power used this hatred to convince Gentiles that every misfortune they have ever suffered in the past was caused by the Jews. The local peasants hated Jews partly because they believed that all Jews are rich. True, most Jewish man and some women in these small towns were better educated than the local population. The Jewish people and their gentile neighbors were also separated by their different customs, their different lifestyles, and their somewhat different traditions. The anti-Semitic laws enacted in the 1930s and 1940s that limited the freedom of Jews, further provoked this hatred.

§ § § § § §

János, as the chief of the local railroad police, was responsible for making sure that law and order was kept in and around the railroad yard and all the surrounding facilities, including a small repair shop. He also made sure that unauthorized personnel were kept away from the trains. The war made this little village busier than it ever was in his lifetime. This area of Hungary contains some of the most fertile land in the country. Even now, after the war finally ended, grains and other foodstuff were being shipped out every day. The Rumanian border was nearby and military personnel were frequently moved back and forth between the two countries.

At around 5 PM, the train with Russian soldiers finally left the station. Most of the day's commotions had died down. By this time, the alcohol had started to take its effect on János. Actually, he felt good because his brain was numbed. As the cool air hit his face, he regained some of his senses and was able to complete his duties as the railroad police chief. His last duty of the day was to check the railroad cars and to make sure that either the cargo was securely locked up or the unloaded ones were completely empty. As he wobbled around the tracks, he heard a faint noise like a small child's cry.

"What is this? Am I hearing things?" He mumbled to himself.

"Even here, I'm hearing those kids!" If someone would watch János, they would notice a somewhat comical expression on his face. After all, a drunk was talking to himself and expecting an answer from a non-existent partner.

"Could I be so drunk, that I'm hearing things?" He shook his head in disbelieve.

"This is not so good, I need to stop drinking!"

János had been married for eight years. He and his wife, Eszti, lived in the village of Békés and he worked in Földvár just a few kilometers away from his home. The couple had four children, between the ages of two and six. He had a small house with two rooms and a kitchen with a pantry. The little ones were always in his way. For the past six years or so, he never had a good night's sleep, but he never complained. He loved his family. During the war, the Hajdú family did not fare too badly. The war had a minimal effect on them. Most military aged men were drafted for the war effort so other than the fact that some young men were missing, the village life was as normal as it could be. Most peasants were poor and worked hard to sustain their life. The family's lonely cow provided enough milk for the family's consumption and they sold the excess milk, cottage cheese, and butter to their neighbors to supplement János's salary from the railroad company, MÁV (Magyar Állami Vasutak).

§ § § § §

His wife, Eszti, took care of the house very well. She got up by sunrise and fed their livestock. Like most families in small towns, the Hajdú family also kept farm animals like chicken, geese, and ducks that provided plenty of eggs and, on special occasions, they became wonderful chicken soup under the masterful hand of Eszti. They would raise at least one pig to provide the family with all the bacon, lard, and sausages that they would need for the rest of the year. Behind the house, there was a vegetable garden providing a supply of peas, carrots, peppers, tomatoes and other vegetables. Several fruit trees provided the family with cherries, prunes, and apples and in the spring strawberries and raspberries. Whatever the family could not consume during the summer, Eszti preserved for the winter and stored them in clear containers that lined the shelves in her pantry.

§§§§§§

As János walked toward the freight cars, the cry of the baby became more and more distinct. Now, he was convinced that indeed he was hearing the cry of a child coming from somewhere near. He spotted a white bundle in one of the open freight cars and when he picked it up, the face of a small baby appeared. The baby was shivering from the cold and was crying because of hunger. János was stunned. He could not believe his own eyes. He often found all sorts of things that were left behind on the trains and had a large collection of those, but a child! During these unstable times, it was rare that these lost items were ever claimed by anyone. Whatever he found useful that was useful, he took ownership of those items, but he had never found anything like a baby!

"What should I do?" He asked himself.

"Where did this baby come from?" He hesitated. He had no idea what to do. He looks around the tracks as if he were looking for someone who could help him. The mother might be nearby and will come back for her baby. Nothing happened. At this time of the day, the railroad yard was completely deserted nobody was around.

"This is so unusual. Never in my life have I faced such a dilemma." His mind was racing for answers. "I cannot even remember anyone telling me a story like this. This is a small town, where practically everyone knew everyone else. Nobody has ever abandoned a baby! Even if a child became orphaned, some family member would take care of the children as they would take care of their very own. This baby must come from another place, perhaps from Budapest, since the train stopped here today came from Budapest."

"Who could do such a desperate deed?" János kept asking himself.

"It is terrible to leave a small child out in the cold." There were no answers from anyone!

"Is anyone out here?" He shouted once more. He was still hoping that the mother might have stepped away for a moment, and maybe she would be back soon. However, nobody answered. Nobody came. The baby was still crying and something had to be done. János still could not believe his eyes. In his half-drunken mind, he was still not sure that this baby was real. Was he daydreaming? The vodka's effect was making this all this seem so real. However, no matter how hard he was trying to dismiss the reality, the bundle was in his hand and the baby was crying. This baby was real!

"What should I do?" He asked himself again and again. His mind was started to clear up and gained his senses.

"I guess I'll have to take you home," he whispered to the baby. The baby just kept crying. János had to make a quick decision. The fact was that the baby needed food, and needed to have his soaking diaper changed. If he did not do something fast, the baby might catch a cold or even pneumonia. He quickly closed his office, get on his bicycle, and peddled home in a hurry.

During the war, all around the country, many children were orphaned. János heard about these unfortunate kids. The crowded orphanages are full of these unfortunate souls. He would not want any kids to have the fate of those poor children. Both he and his wife loved children. János figured that having one more child in his family would not make too much of a difference in their life. János knew that his wife, Eszti would not easily accept this bundle, but after all, he was the man of the house, and he would not let her talk him out of this. Now he felt good about taking this poor baby home. By the time he got to his house, he also made the decision to keep the baby away from the local authorities.

János, with all his faults, was still a responsible person and he took his job and his life seriously. The baby's future now looked promising now that János had found him. Others might have made a different decision and the baby's future would have been completely different. János decision to give a home to this helpless child permanently changed the future of this orphan. The baby could have died on the train. The baby could have ended up in an orphanage and been lost among the hundreds of other homeless children. The baby would have grown up in a different environment with a different future and completely different life.

§ § § § §

I know this is a slight detour from my story. It is necessary for you, the reader, to understand the consequences of this event. We all know that G-d works in mysterious ways. Moreover, this story may serve as another proof of this theory. This baby was left on the train by a mother, whose faith we do not know and we can only speculate what actually happened to her. Why would a mother abandon her child? Why? Acts like these occur only in desperate times and circumstances beyond our understanding. The strength of motherhood could rarely be weakened to a level that makes a mother give up something as precious as a child. Even if a mother had to give up her child, she would surely see to her child's safety and leave the baby somewhere safe, not in a cold unattended railroad car. Probably, she could not take care of this fragile baby the way she wanted to. She was hoping that some Good Samaritan might find him and take care of him the way she would never be able to do. The Russian Red Army was well known for their atrocities against civilians; thousands of women and girls were raped. Probably, the Russians did not want a woman with a baby and forcibly took the baby away from her. Despite themselves, they may have saved the baby's life by putting him into the empty wagon. Possibly, she was killed at the brutal hands of these barbarians. Probably…who knows? Nobody will ever know how this baby ended up in a railroad car in Földvár.

§ § § § § §

As expected, Eszti was not amused when János got home with the baby. For now, she changed the baby's diaper; they saw the baby was a boy, about 8 to 10 months old. There was something else strange that she noticed. The boy was circumcised! This procedure was rare in Hungary in those days and even today. The only time non-Jewish boys were circumcised was when there was an infection and circumcision was unavoidable so the child would be able urinating. The fact that Jewish boys were circumcised helped the Nazis to identify Jewish men when they could not find any other means to reveal their Jewish identities.

"Is it possible he is Jewish?" Eszti asked János.

"I don't know," he replied, "perhaps, he is." János continued, "I know that Jewish boys are circumcised; I guess he must be Jewish."

"Well as far as I know, there are no Jews left in this town," Eszti finally said, "let's just keep him for a while." She paused and continued. "We will determine what to do with him later."

After the baby drank some milk, he stopped crying. Eszti put him on the bed and he comfortably went to sleep. The baby was quite nice looking. He had a round face with beautiful blue eyes. Their heart was opened to accept him. The couple was talking for a while about this baby. This baby was a gift from G-d. For some reason, they believed that G-d had kept his eye on this boy and sent him to János. G-d knew that even though the Hajdú family did not have much money, they were good people and they would take care of this boy as their very own. They were discussing what this new member of their family would do to the family finances. They both agreed that for now, everything would be fine. Enough hand-me-downs from their other children would fit him. The extra milk and any other food for this little boy would not cause any financial problems for the family budget.

"I'm worried about the authorities," Eszti said. "What happens if they find out about this baby and they take him away?"

"I think we should talk to Dr. Pintér, the lawyer and ask him for his advice." János finally answered after a short silence. They agreed that in the next day or so, János would seek the advice of Dr. Pintér. At least someone who understands the law could advise them how to keep this baby legally.

The next day the couple went to see Dr. Pintér. They told him the events of the previous day and their intention of keeping the baby.

§ § § § § §

Dr. Lajos Pintér was a charming old man, well respected in his community. He helped poor people with their problems even without asking for money. It is not often one can encounter this rare behavior. Dr. Pintér had been practicing law for over 30 years that provided a comfortable life for him and for his family. He stayed away from politics and remained in the background in order to avoid problems during times of turmoil.

When the Hajdú family came to him, he understood their concerns and encouraged them to keep the baby. He also noted that the boy was possibly Jewish, and perhaps one day, someone might come to claim him. Before the war, he had many Jewish friends and was one of the gentiles who felt their pain, and tried to help them as much as he could without getting himself into any troubles.

"I could obtain a birth certificate for him. It would be better if I take care of the paperwork. This way the police will not bother you with questions."

"I have some connections with the town's administration. I know the mayor of the town." Dr. Pintér continued after he made some notations. "Do you know what to call him, yet?"

"I like the name Lacika," Eszti said, "I guess we can call him László"

"We need a last name," Dr. Pintér reminded his clients. "We should not register him with your last name. We do not want to falsify his identity"

"We found him in Földvár." Eszti said, "so we could name him László Földvári."

It was settled. The baby had a new identity, a new life, and a renewed hope for his future. They all agreed that Dr. Pintér would be his official guardian and the Hajdú family would be his foster parents. Dr. Pintér would take care of all paperwork for the registration of the baby with the authorities and the Hajdú family would take care of the baby for a while. They also discussed the possibility of adoption, but they had to be confident that nobody would come forward claiming the baby. Until then, Lacika would stay with the loving care of the Hajdú family.

At least for now…he will stay.

2

the woman

When Helen was young, she had a comfortable life with her parents in Nagydobos, a small village in eastern Hungary. Her father owned a general store, where the village peasants would buy various dry goods. These poor working people often had no money or not enough money to pay for the goods they bought at her father's store. In those days, it was quite customary for storeowners like Helen's father to keep a ledger to track items people had purchased throughout the year. It was understood that the people of the village would pay whenever they could, mostly after the fall harvest. Until then, he kept careful records of their purchases and eventually he was paid; at least most of the time. In 1930, Helen's father lost most of his money due to the worldwide recession caused by the World War I. People, his trusted neighbors, had no money to pay for all that they purchased during the year. Unfortunately, his creditors demanded their money. Her father lost his store, his source of income; he had hard time accepting his loss. He became ill, so sick that could no longer work. The total loss of income took a heavy toll on the family finances.

In the 1930s, the expectation for young women, especially Jewish ones, was to get married, have children, and to take care of her husband and children. Unfortunately, for Helen, this life style was not in her immediate future. Helen was the oldest unmarried child of her large family. Out of the nine siblings, three were still living at home with their parents. Her other siblings were married and had moved away with their respective spouses and were living their own life. Her mother, father, and three younger siblings needed financial help. Helen took charge and she became a seamstress. She hoped that having a trade and finding a job would get her enough income to support her family and could provide her parents and siblings a comfortable life and a life of dignity for her. One of the family's friends had a store in Mátészalka, a larger town nearby, and invited Helen to share their storefront with her. Helen moved to Mátészalka in 1931. Inside the friend' store, she opened a salon for custom made girdles and bras.

Years of illness took its toll on her father and he died in 1934. Helen had learned her profession very well. The money that she was able to make was enough to cover her own modest expenses and was able to provide a comfortable life for her mother and all her siblings, until…

§ § § § § §

Hitler attacked Poland in September 1, 1939 and the World War II "officially" started. In late 1939, Helen got married to Ede. What timing to get married! Ede wanted to immigrate to the USA. The American quota for Hungarian emigration was limited; on the other hand, the Czechoslovakian quota was wide open, since the economy of this country was much better than economies of Hungary. Ede's plan was to become Czechoslovakian citizen and gain entry to the USA. Unfortunately, his plan did not work out, because Hitler decided to give back some territories lost by the Hungarians, his allies, after WW I, and Ede found himself back in Hungary. Almost immediately after this event, Ede was drafted into the army and served in the Forced Labor Service. The newlyweds were separated; they had seen each other only a few times before they both ended up in various concentration camps.

§ § § § § §

What could Helen do? Her family still needed her help. She stayed in Mátészalka and continued working to support her mother and her siblings. By 1943, more and more Jewish laws had forced Jews to give up their business; Helen had to move back to Nagydobos with her mother and her younger siblings. All this time, she had no idea where her husband was. At this point, she was not even sure that her husband was still alive; but the worst was yet to come.

The year was 1944, more than a year had passed since the German army, and the Axis powers (armies of Hungarians, Romanians, and Italians) were defeated at Stalingrad. The Red Army pushed hard and the attacking German armies were forced to retreat leaving behind thousands and thousands of dead and wounded. Among them were their own military personnel along with many more thousands of civilian casualties of the local population. "D Day" had still not made history, there were months to go before the Allied Forces would launch a massive attack on German forces. The Germans were clearly losing the war on both fronts; especially from the east, the Russians were pushing hard and from the west, the English and the Americans were getting ready to move. Despite all these setbacks, the trains carrying Jews and other "non-desirables" were given priority to reach their destinations. The Germans wasted precious fuel, manpower, and money for this cause. Hitler and his deranged followers believed that the killing of Jews was more important than winning the war. The Germans probably suffered more casualties because trains were carrying Jews to concentration camps instead of supplying badly needed weapons, ammunitions, and medication to their own solders.

In April 1944, like most Jewish families in the area, Helen's family was rounded up by the Nazis with the help of their Hungarian collaborators. They were moved into a transit camp. In early June, Helen and her family were sent to Auschwitz. Her family, along with many of their fellow Jewish men, women, and children, were crowded into cattle cars. We all know about the good organization skills of the Germans; they did a "good job" emptying out all the Hungarian villages of unwanted Jews. The efficient German military personnel packed as many people into each wagon as they could and more. The only crime "committed" by these desperate, unfortunate people was that they were Jewish. Stripped of their dignity and pride, they had hardly enough space to sit on the filthy floor of the cattle cars. Occasionally during their weeklong trip, the guards gave them some tasteless soup and stale bread to eat; just enough food so that most of the people would survive the long trip. These people had never seen nor could they ever imagine the horror that was waiting for them at the end of their trip. Many died at the brutal hands of their guards, as well as from starvation and illness. There was no attempt by the Nazis to save anyone on the train. When the guards found dead bodies, they simply tossed them off the cars. Why bother to bury them? There was no time to waste; the Nazis were in a hurry to kill as many Jews as they could.

It was a beautiful early-summer day, but the passengers of the "luxury compartments" of the cattle-cars were not enjoying their ride. They were hungry, sick, and exhausted from the weeklong dreadful trip. To their horror, an unforeseen delay occurred along the road leading to Auschwitz. The delay was caused by an "unscheduled" air attack. The mission was ordered by Air Chief Marshal Harris of the British Royal Air Force (RAF) to attack railroad lines to slow down military supply routes. Unfortunately, the RAF did not do a perfect job of destroying the railroad tracks leading to Auschwitz. Shortly after the attack, the guards made a quick assessment of the train, they made sure that all cars are securely locked, removed most of the dead bodies they noticed, and started to move the train again. The sun had already set by the time Helen and the others got off the train at gates of hell: Auschwitz. Getting off the train, Helen could not believe her ears! She heard music. A band was playing beautiful, cheery, classical music as if they were in an outdoor concert. Voices from loudspeakers in German, Hungarian, Polish, and Russian were assuring the new arrivals that their relocation was now completed.

"There is no reason to be frightened."

"The worst is over and you have reached your final destination and you have arrived to your new home…"

Yes, the phrase "final destination" was correct for most arrivals. Helen walked along with the others through a large iron gate. On the other side of the gate, the sound of music disappeared and the most horrifying place in the world, Auschwitz, was revealed. It felt as if their hearts stopped. The smell of burning flesh filled the air.

A tall, handsome man in a white coat, the kind of man that could make a women's heart pound, was standing near the gate. Dr. Mengele, the "Angel of Death," was personally directing the "human traffic," and made instant decisions about people; either immediate death or more suffering that would eventually lead to death. He pointed to children and their mothers, the old and the sick move to the left and the stronger people to the right. Men and women, husbands and wives were also separated.

"Please do not do this to us," people screamed with terror. The guards replied only with their sticks, hitting those who had fallen, hitting those who would not move fast enough. How could anyone move fast? They were exhausted, they were desperate, they were weak from hunger and thirst, and they felt confused and hopeless. It seemed that the SS guards enjoyed their brutality; they were hitting everyone in their reach… The real horror started or rather was continued.

"Why are you taking our wives and children away?" many men tried to ask their cruel guards, but the answers were more beatings. The beatings continued beyond all reason by the human trash called SS Guards.

"Why are you taking our husbands away?" Cries of women were heard from all over. Who ever talked was beaten by the guards. People cried out of fear and frustration, but their guards showed absolutely no mercy.

Since the transport arrived late, the guards were rushing the registration and separation of the prisoners. The night settled in, some of the exhausted people fell asleep; some just lied down and wondered what would happen the next day. Would they wake up from this horrible dream? What would tomorrow bring? Is there a tomorrow for them? The camp became eerily quiet, only the white smoke stacks from the incinerators were visible on the dark clear sky above.

Like many others, the trip to Auschwitz made Helen sick. She felt horrible by the time she got off the train. In the "selection" process, she was told to go left along with the sick and old. People on the left were destined for the gas chambers. Helen did not know this. The only thing she felt was that she ended up in this group because she looked very ill. She could not predict her future staying where she was at this point, but...

The strong will to survive had always helped Helen. Somehow, she felt that she was on the wrong side! Did a "right side" exist?" She felt she must do something, even though, at this time, Helen had no clue that she was doomed for the gas chambers. She somehow felt that staying here would not be the right place to be. For the rest of her life, Helen never understood why she had this feeling, but this feeling and her determination saved her life. In the middle of the night, she kissed her mother goodbye, whom she would never see again; she perished in the gas chambers and incinerators. She kept low and slowly but surely inched her way to the first barrack she had seen. She had terrible pains all over her body, but she kept going ignoring all the pains. The dark night became her partner and helped her to succeed. She crawled into the building and pretended as if she belonged to this group. Some people grunted at her and moved over to make some space for her to lie down.

"Helen!" Someone whispered. She looked around, but could not see the caller in the dark.

"Helen, look over here!" The voice called again. She maneuvered herself toward the voice. To her amazement, Helen recognized Bözsi, one of her husband's sisters. Happiness is a weird thing; finding a familiar face, even if the person had never been kind to her. In these desperate times, a small joy was overwhelming.

"How long have you been here?" Helen asked her.

"Ibi, Aranka, and I got here two days ago." Bözsi replied, "let us hope we can stay together." In their misery, Helen and her sister-in-laws were happy to see each other. In the past, the sister-in-laws had never liked her, but never the less, the four women managed to stay together for more than 10 months until their liberation.

§ § § § § §

The resentment between the sister-in-laws and Helen started years ago. We have to go back in time, to the time before Ede and Helen even knew each other, way before they had gotten married. Ede's father had a small dry goods store selling everything from textiles to haberdashery and other dry goods. He made a decent living, but he was not rich at all. How could he be? He had ten children: five boys and five girls. Enough mouths to feed, dress, and educate. Without a sizable dowry, a middle class Jewish girl had little chance to marry into another middle class family in the 1920s and 1930s. Ede's father could not afford a reasonable dowry for all five girls. The family made a strategic decision, a pact: After one of the boys got married, part of his new wife's dowry would be used to supplement one of his sisters' dowries, so they too could marry well. Many families made similar arrangements. Ede broke this tradition and the three unmarried sisters have never forgiven Helen for this.

"You had the nerve to marry a poor woman without a dowry." The girls would tell Ede too many times. "Who could believe nowadays to get married for love, not for money?" They would annoy Ede with this for many years to come. The three unmarried sisters were unforgiving; they got married after the war, but still the Kupferstein girls never accepted Helen. Even in the horrors of Auschwitz, these women would not treat Helen any better than one would treat a servant. Nevertheless, Helen had a strong sense of family that helped her through these hard times.

§ § § § § §

Helen never had the tattooed numbers on her arm as most people were given in Auschwitz. A few days after Helen arrived in Auschwitz, she and her in-laws were transferred to Birkenau, the largest of all sub-camps of Auschwitz. Birkenau was the camp where the Nazis murdered more prisoners, Jews, gypsies, communists, and other "undesirables" than in any of the other death camps. This camp was a combination of labor camp and death camp, but mostly death camp. Some stronger, healthier people were "selected" to perform hard labor in various factories or in farms.

The winter of 1944 arrived early. It was the worst winter anyone could remember in a long time. The inmates were very poorly, fed and clothed their sanitary conditions were disasters. A civilized person cannot even imagine how a human being could be treated in this manner. The freezing cold made these people's lives even more miserable. The cruel guards made people stand, sometime naked, in the cold, freezing weather to be counted. More often than not, there were inconsistencies and they let people go back to their barracks only when they had counted everyone again and again they had found everyone dead or alive. The cold and malnutrition took a toll on all, and many died during these "counting." Dead bodies were everywhere. Other inmates were ordered to pick up these cold, poorly clothed, miserable bodies, put them into a cart and carry them to an area where the bodies were disposed. The furnaces were working 24 hours a day. Many among the living wished to be dead, where there would be no more misery, no more punishments, and no more suffering. They were hoping for tranquility. Tomorrow might bring some hope, but most of them did not believe there was a future. Many did not believe that they would be able to survive all this. Most of those who had this pessimistic view indeed did not survive, only a few lucky ones did. Were they lucky? Who are we to say? I was not alive then, I can only say what I heard and read from survivors. This topic is controversial and I would defer to people who know better.

One miserable morning, a couple of months into their misery, Helen and most of the women in her barrack were lined up and without any explanations; they were marched out of the camp. Everyone feared that this might be the end, but it was not. The women were boarded on a train; a train just like the one that had brought them here, but now they were being taken somewhere else. The two-day long journey took them to another camp. Many did not survive the trip and they were disposed of the way Nazis routinely had done. This camp, Bromberg-Ost, was part of the larger group of concentration camps named Stutthof, somewhat lesser known, but one of the first of its kind. Maybe this camp was a little better than Auschwitz/Birkenau, but it still was a concentration camp. This camp was a work camp for women only. Inside the camp, most of the guards were women, but their superiors were SS men. The majority of the inmates were Polish Jews and other Polish "non-desirables." Helen and her in-laws were among the few Hungarians. The Polish inmates would not accept them, because they were angry about the fact that the Hungarians had a "good-time" while the Polish Jews were already in these camps for years. After a few weeks, the four women were transferred again to another camp near the city Thorn (Polish name Torun).

Helen was 37 years old. It was a miracle that she survived these harsh conditions. The inmates, mostly women, were digging huge holes in the middle of a pine forest. These holes were supposed to be tank traps. Helen always wondered how any tank could get into these beautiful, very dense forests. What would they do there? Why would they go there? In any other times, this forest would be so peaceful. The work assignment would be extremely hard for anyone, but was much harder for women. Helen had never performed any heavy physical work before, her muscles were not designed to perform this kind of work; but her strong will, the will to live, helped Helen to survive.

In late March 1945, the Soviet Red Army liberated the camp. Among the prisoners, many Russian prisoners were sharing the same fate as the Jews. The Russians mostly helped only the Russian prisoners, others were somewhat ignored. Several days after the liberation, the Red Cross set up medical facilities to help those who were most in need. Many sick women were taken to Sweden by Swedish social workers. The Swedes wanted to help these women to restart their life, heal their wounds, teach them trade, and welcome them back to the human race. The Swedes did a great job of helping many Jewish women who had survived the terrors of the Holocaust. These women have learned new trades and learned one of the most important thing in life is to feel like useful human beings again.

Helen and her sister-in-laws were not sure what to do or where to go after they gained their freedom. Helen did not want to go to a strange land like Sweden or America. She wanted to go home, where she hoped to find peace again and hoped to find her husband, her family, and her friends. A few weeks after the liberation, the four women left the camp. They needed some time to gain back some of their strength before they could start the long journey home. Nobody told them how to get back home, what direction to take, what to do next. During the first few days, the four women were just wondering around. When they were hungry, they walked into the nearest Polish village or farm. Most local Polish people were not too friendly toward strangers, especially Jewish strangers. Their situation was further complicated, because none of them spoke Polish. The winter cold was still around and their garments were not warm enough to protect them from the elements. To get back home, they need something warmer than the rags they been wearing ever since the liberation. Finally, a local peasant family felt pity on these lost women and gave them some food and an old coat, a scarf, an old shoe. Nobody was hospitable enough to invite these Jews into their homes.

These women had no clue which direction to go. One day, they spotted a stationary long freight train standing still on the open field. The four managed get into one of the open wagons. Getting on the freight train gave them chills, remembering their trip many months ago. They hoped the train would go south, the direction of Hungary. The train took off and their journey began to the unknown. In the middle of the night, the train arrived at a large train station. As the workers were checking the train, Helen and the sisters were discovered and they were chased off the train.

"Where are we? Helen asked the others, but had no clue.

"I am sure we are still in Poland. We did not travel long enough." Aranka made an educated guess.

"We should look around and someone might be able to tell us where we are." Helen was proposing some plan of action. The four women were scared, but they walked to the station building and the station sign read Bromberg. The city's original Polish name was Bydgoszcz as they later discovered.

"At least we know the name of the city." One of them tried to be funny. "Of course, I never heard of this city before, nor I have any idea where this city is located on the map, but I have never been good in geography."

The platform of the station was completely deserted with the exception of these four lost women. Slowly the daylight arrived and they could clearly see that this city was a large city. Bromberg sounded German, but they did not know if they were in Poland or in Germany. The lost women did not speak Polish, but Helen spoke Yiddish and she tried to ask for help from people walking by. Most people spoke German in this area of Poland, but they would not stop. Finally, they came across an older man, who was willing to listen to Helen and brought them to a local Jewish organization. Helen explained to the people that they were liberated more than a month ago by the Russians from the camp near Torun. Of course, they had neither passports nor any identification documents. Even without Helen's explanation, the people at the organization could clearly see the evidence of sufferings on the faces of the four lost women. Anyone just had to look at them and immediately could tell who they were.

The entire building was set up to help displaced Jewish refugees. The facility provided room and board for the four women, and they been offered a place to stay as long as they wished. After what Helen and the sister-in-laws went through, the place was like heaven. Except for Helen, who had some infection for which the doctor prescribed some medication, their health was reasonably good. For the first time in a long time, they felt like normal human beings again. They were able to take a long, hot, relaxing bath with real soap. They were given some used, but clean dresses, comfortable shoes, and warm coats. In addition, a medical doctor gave them a thorough examination to assess their health. The four women could hardly recognize each other in their fresh, clean clothing. When dinner came, hot, nourishing food was served, with seconds if they wanted to eat more. Most residents were fellow survivors, mostly from Poland. No other Hungarians were staying there.

After a few weeks of relaxing time, Helen and her in-laws felt much better, stronger, and somewhat happier. They were able to walk again freely on the streets observing life start getting back to "normal," they took some trips outside the town and at the first time in their life has seen the ocean, where Helen collected some seashells and brought them home. The four women started to get restless; they felt the urge to move on, but, where to go? People at the Jewish organization were encouraging them to go to Sweden. However, Helen was still hesitating. She truly wanted to go home, but she was afraid to face the hard reality. As many questions she have asked herself, as many were left without any answers.

"Did any of my loved ones survived?"

"What should I do, if none of them come back?"

"How would I be able to start my life again all alone?"

"Would I have enough strength to survive by myself?" She had no misconceptions; she knew that most of her relatives had perished. She was hoping though that her husband, or some of her eight siblings, or some of her numerous cousins survived. She knew that she could not rely on her in-laws, no matter how much suffering they had endured together. Unlike the three sisters, she still had her profession and she could reopen her salon.

By late spring, Helen and the three sisters finally made their decision to go home. The Jewish agency gave them some traveling money. Their long journey towards home started. They managed to get home with various means of transportation: by traveling on foot, on crowded trains, catching a bus, hitching on a horse-drawn cart and any other means of transportation they were able to find. During their trip, they crossed through war torn Poland, Czechoslovakia, and Hungary, crossing the path of hundreds and thousands of displaced people going in all directions to all destinations. The war was not really over yet and trains were scarce and overcrowded. The trip back home took them over a month. Helen and her sister-in-laws parted ways; Helen went back to her parents' house in Nagydobos and the sisters went to Kisvárda to their fathers' house.

Helen after the liberation was merely 35 kilos (70 lb). It took months before Helen started to gain back some weight and started to look like a human being again. Six months later, she still could not recognize herself in the mirror. Her hair started to grow back but her face still showed the tremendous suffering she endured during her stay in the concentration camps. When she got home, she found her brother Icú. Helen found out that her sister Rózsi somehow ended up in Budapest, where she survived in one of the Swedish safe houses. Rózsi decided not to move back to Nagydobos and stayed in her apartment in Budapest. Most of Helen's immediate family, including her mother, four brothers, two sisters and their families had perished in Auschwitz and other death camps.

The hope of finding loved ones was strong among the survivors. After returning from the camps, most everyone was waiting for the return of their loved ones, but as time went by many lost hope to see their loved ones ever again. In their hearts, most of them knew that they would never see most of their family members ever again. After a while, many gave up waiting. Many either moved to nearby larger cites from villages or made their decision just like Icú had done; to move to either to Palestine or to many other parts of the world where they hoped for a brighter, better future than what they may face in Hungary. For months, Helen lived with her brother, Icú in her parents' old house until the summer of 1946, when Icú got married and immigrated to Palestine. He as many concentration camp survivors, made the decision not to stay in Hungary and wanted to go and build a new homeland for the Jewish people. Helen was still hoping. Only a handful of married couples survived the terrors of the concentration camps. For long months, it seemed that her husband had perished just as many others did.

3

the man

"How long this could go on?"

"Why us?"

"How long this will go on?"

"Why always us?"

"Are we ever going to survive these horrors?"

"What did we do to deserve this?"

These and other thoughts were on the minds of the "residents" of Mauthausen camp. Of course, this camp was not created for young children, who were sent to spend and enjoy their summer vacations. By no means was it, not at all!

It was the spring of 1945 and the war was nearing to its end. Almost a year ago, the Allied invasion of Normandy on June 6, 1944, better known as the "D Day," had destroyed most of Germany's military might, but the residents of this camp had no idea about what was happening in the outside world. Their suffering seemed endless.

Finally, the hardest winter in many years came to end. It was early May and the sun was trying hard to warm up the air in and around the row of barracks. These barracks were lined up on both sides of the main road connecting the main gate with the rest of the camp. The bright sun was not able to make the lives of the detainees any better. The soil of the camp was still partly frozen. The warm sun started to thaw the frozen ground and morphed it into a muddy mixture of soil and the accumulated grime; filthy rubbish that had collected during the past few years that nobody ever tried to clean up. There was no reason to clean it since every day more, and more human-waste, blood, sweat and tears accumulated on the ground. The "management" of the camp did not care about the conditions of the "facilities." German SS (Schutzstaffel) was the management. Uncollected dead bodies were lying all over the camp and the open pits of latrines were spreading an awful stench into the air.

Nobody ever willingly spent time in this place or in a number of other concentration camps like this or were even worse than this. Unfortunate people who found themselves on the wrong side of the prejudiced society, ended up in here, mostly Jews and other "undesirables" including a large contingent of Russian soldiers. Thousands were already dead, and many more would die under these conditions. Thus far, there was no end in sight. The conditions in these camps were worst than any civilized human being could ever imagine. Only in the minds of the Nazis were these horrible, inhumane conditions and treatment of people justified.

The Nazis used any means to break the spirit of these imprisoned, innocent people. The inmates had to work hard otherwise the guards made their life even more miserable. Was it possible to be worst than this? Yes, many that survived testified about this. Mauthausen was a work camp, or the way the Germans call it "Vernichtung durch Arbeit" (extermination by work). In Mauthausen, the Germans did not have any special facilities to exterminate the inmates unlike the camps designated as death camps like Auschwitz/Birkenau, Treblinka, Sobibor and Belzec. Of course, the standard components of a small gas chamber and a crematorium were part of the main campground, how could a concentration camp be without these? The harsh conditions, lack of medical care and the severe winter cold have done the work of killing thousands. As a token of "appreciation" for their work, the guards gave these people some hard, stale bread and tasteless lean soup containing mostly hot water with the occasional potatoes or sugar beets. Certainly, the food provided was hardly enough to sustain their health and provide enough energy to work and was not enough to survive the hard winter. The Nazis did not want the detainees to survive. Many of the poor souls were walking around like living skeletons.

The SS guards appointed the stronger inmates, both Jews and non-Jews, to be responsible for a group of people. Their jobs were to keep their fellow inmates in line and to do some of the dirty work that even the SS guards would not do. These people were commonly called the "Capo," a term borrowed from the Italian "capo regime" used by the mafia for their high-ranking bosses. These capos were forced to carry out horrible deeds and in return, they got a false hope that this cooperation would save their miserable lives a bit longer. It gave them a small sense of hope to survive this horror and be able to tell the world about their survival. Only a few of these capos would help their fellow Jews. If the SS guards would see a capo showing any mercy to his fellow inmates, the guards would severely punish and in most cases would not hesitate to kill the disobeying capo.

§ § § § § §

Ede was born and grown up in small town called Kisvárda located in the Northeast of Hungary. He was a graduate of gymnasium. Gymnasium, in the Hungarian education system, was a form of high school emphasizing classical languages and literature. In the 1920s, very few people finished high school, unlike the number of high school graduates in late twentieth century. High school educated people were considered "well educated" people in the early part of the twentieth century. Only a privileged few, mostly children of the wealthy or a few exceptionally talented students from the lower classes, were able to attend these schools. Entrance into higher education institutions like Universities was limited to the upper class, for anyone else it was almost unattainable. The "Numerous Clausus," a quota system, enacted in 1920, defined the maximum number of Jewish students allowed to attend Universities. This law limited the number of Jews allowed to attend higher education institutions to six percent; same percentage as the Jewish population of Hungary. Prior to the quota system, between 25 to 40 percent of all university students were Jewish. Many talented Jewish kids were deprived of higher education due to these ridiculous entry quotas.

Shortly after his graduation from the gymnasium, Ede was drafted into the Hungarian army. Until the late 1920s, Jewish and non-Jewish military age young men were drafted into the same units of the Military. Ede was automatically given a rank of lieutenant, earned by his level of education. Before the restricting Jewish laws of the 1930s were enacted, gentiles and Jews were serving alongside each other in the military as equals. In the late 1930s, many humiliating Jewish laws were legislated by Hungarian government, imitating some of the measures that Hitler's Germany enacted against their own Jewish population. Fortunately, in the beginning, thanks to Miklós Horthy, Regent of Hungary, these restrictions were not as severe as they were in Germany. However, the rights of Jewish citizens kept being taken away slowly, and after the German army occupied Hungary on March 19, 1944, Jews had no rights at all.

At first, Jews were limited where they could work and whom they could employ. By the end of 1939, Jews were isolated from the rest of the population. Jewish men were no longer allowed to server in the military forces, which of course was not a great loss for anyone. The Hungarians were allies of Germany, and the German leadership demanded maximum manpower for the war effort. The Hungarian government, as an ally, had a certain amount of independence within its borders and Hitler did not directly interfere with the Hungarians dealings with its Jewish population. After the war broke out in 1939, all military age men, including the Jews, were drafted into the Hungarian army. Hungarians, unlike their German counterparts, implemented an unusual idea: Jews would serve in the military not as soldiers, but as laborers and utility workers. The anti-Semitic government would not trust Jews anymore. The military would not issue weapons to any Jew, not even to their officers. These Jewish units were organized the same way as the regular military units were, but Jewish officers were reporting to their Christian counterparts. The Jewish units were responsible for building roads, bridges and performing any labor-intensive work that was essential in helping the military's war efforts. Ede was drafted into the 122nd Hungarian Royal Railroad Builder Regiment and served as lieutenant, getting back his original military rank awarded to him before the war. He and his unit were ordered to the Russian front and ended up near Stalingrad.

§ § § § § §

February 1943 was the turning point of World War II. In and around Stalingrad, the Russians, with the help of the extreme cold Russian-winter, stopped the German advances. The reinforced army of the Soviet Union's Red Army was thrashing the mighty German Sixth Army and the Second Hungarian army. The Hungarian army took a severe beating at the bend of the Don River and they lost more than 80% of their military personnel, numbered in the tens of thousands people. After the defeat, Ede was retreating with his unit along with the beaten remnant of the Hungarian Second army. With the Red Army on their tails, the Hungarian army was in chaos. Their retreat was complicated by the harsh winter and they lost many, many more men, Jews, and non-Jews alike.

§ § § § § §

After months of walking in the freezing cold winter, finally, Ede and his people were back on Hungarian soil. Ede with some of his Jewish friends wanted to disappear from the army. Ede with the help of his gentile friend, a sergeant from Kisvárda, made an escape plan. They were serving in the same army unit and this made their planning easier. The plan was simple plan: Ede's sergeant friend would pretend to be a "prison guard," transporting "Jewish deserters" to somewhere. The location of "somewhere" was changed constantly as they traveled further west into Hungary. Deserters in those days were usually shot without asking any questions, without any trials. This small group took a dangerous chance, but everyone was fed up with this crazy war and wanted to go home already. They had some success in evading the military police.

Unfortunately, their desertion tactic did not end up working out as well as they had hoped. They did not have any official, valid military orders to prove their mission. The group was captured again and again, sometimes by the Hungarians and sometimes by the Germans. The Red Army was pushing hard. Day and night, the small group heard the sounds of artillery getting closer and closer. Their captors never had enough time to execute them due to the ongoing hard push by the Red Army. The group got smaller each time they were captured, because not everyone in the group was captured, some were able to hide before the group was discovered. After a few times they were captured, no more escape was possible. This time, Ede's sergeant friend got away, but the rest were captured and attached to a Jewish transport. The Germans, while they were fleeing for their own life, the growing numbers of Jewish inmates were forced to walk all the way to Mauthausen.

Ede arrived to Mauthausen, a concentration camp in Austria, with one of the last transports that reached Mauthausen from Hungary. Since he spoke perfect German and was in charge of fellow Jews as a lieutenant, he was appointed as a capo. The word "capo" had very bad connotations. Ede was one of those few who risked their own life to help their fellow Jews to survive. Unlike other capos, Ede tried his best to save his fellow Jews from certain death. During the two long months in the Mauthausen concentration camp, Ede gained the reputation as the "good capo" and fellow Jews tried to join his group. Two of his fellow inmates later married Ede's sisters and they became his brother-in-laws. The two men assumed that any sister of this kind man would be just as kind of a person as their brother was.

Bright sunshine woke up the inmates, not the usual brutal hands of the SS guards. The camp was unusually quiet on this morning of May 5, 1945. Overnight, the guards kept the barracks locked. In the mornings, the guards would wake up their prisoners by loudspeaker to get the inmates ready to go to work. Today, the guards broke their daily routine; the loudspeakers were silent. It was quiet all morning, too quiet. Some inmates carefully peaked out from the window and spotted a few guards in the distance. The guards were simply standing around without doing anything. At first, everyone braced for the "beginning of the end." These desperate people were almost sure that they had reached the end of their journey and today might be the day when the Nazis would kill them all.

They were wrong. They were all wrong...

What can they lose, more and more people tried to assess the situation and some even climbed out the window to have a closer look at the main gate. Normally by the main gate, guards were stationed with their machine guns. However, this time, none of them could be seen anywhere. This was very suspicious, unexplainable, and unbelievable, but quite frightening. Most everyone stayed in the barracks. In the past, the guards would never tolerate any rest like this; there were no weekends, there were no holidays, there were no rest, only suffering was allowed. The inmates could never stay inside their barracks during the day. Their guards always found a reason to make them get out. Today, the prisoners found another thing to be unusually strange: there was no distribution of food. The food had never been any good or enough, but with German efficiency, the food was always delivered promptly.

"What is this?"

"What is going on?" People started to ask each other.

"Are we all going to die today?"

Uncertainty is considered worse than knowing the truth, even when the truth was painful. Had the "final solution" succeeded for these people and they would all be killed?

"NO, NO! It cannot be." Others were shouting with panic.

"Could this quiet mean the end of Germans?" Some would dare to speculate.

"Would this be the end of our misery?" An anticipation of hope was in the air.

"Please be it!"

Today, for the first time in a long time, inmates started to hope, hope for better things to come.

Around noon, even a stranger thing occurred. A Jeep carrying a single American soldier drove through the main gate with an automatic weapon lying by the driver's feet for easy reach. He started to yell something in English that Ede did not understand, most people did not understand. A few minutes later, more Americans arrived.

The barrack doors were opened by the American soldiers and they kept assuring the prisoners in broken German.

"Alles ein Ende haben.—It is all over."

"Alles freikommen.—You are all free!"

"Everyone can go home whenever they wish to go." It took some time until these hopeless people finally realized what was happening to them! It was hard to believe that after all the suffering the doors of Mauthausen camp were opened and their suffering was over. Was it true they were all free? The solders started to distribute all kinds of food, cigarettes, and candies. FOOD! Real food, lots of good food.

"Please take it easy with the food." The soldiers kept warning them.

"Please, you need not worry. There is enough food for everyone and even more." The Americans kept telling the people to slow down. It was so hard to resist food! One cannot even imagine how these people felt at these moments. They were seeing real food for the first time in many months or years. For them, what happened today seemed almost unreal, like waking up from a nightmare, but not completely gaining back your conscience and still being under the influence of the nightmare.

"Please, eat slowly. Do not eat too much at one time." The Americans kept asking them, but very few people were listening to these warnings. They were too hungry and too tired to understand and realize the seriousness of these warnings. The soldiers already knew how dangerous it was for these sick and weakened people to eat too much at first. They have seen too many die while having food in their mouths due to the shock to their weakened body.

"I think there are some SS still around," someone shouted. "I have seen some of them earlier." Someone else joined in.

"Let us get them," others shouted. These desperate people had the anger, but not the strength to do what they wanted to do. It was as if someone waived a magic wand and suddenly gave unbelievable strength to many. Some were running, some were walking, some were crawling, but whoever could move, tried to move as fast as they could. The angry mob got into the guard's barrack sand the SS guards did not resist. Yesterday nobody could have imagined and would not have believed this could happen. Without hesitation, the scared Nazis were dragged out from hiding. The 30 or so guards were hiding they did not have enough the time to flee. These angry people were gabbing anything that they could use to hurt them. The used a piece of rock, a stick of wood or used their bare hands and before the American's could intervene, most of the guards were beaten to a pulp by the prisoners and died almost instantaneously. The rest of these despicable people were shot by their own guns. Some were emptying their guns with such anger that they had never experienced in their lives. Years of suffering had taken a toll on people's nerves. Killing the guards who terrorized them gave a certain level of satisfaction to the inmates.

Days passed after the liberation. The Red Cross set up a large tent for a hospital in addition to the hospital ward of the camp. Most of the people needed some kind of medical help. Many had contracted typhus and other diseases; their bodies had weakened due to malnutrition, beatings, and tortures. Only a few were able to leave within a few days. The Americans did their best to help the ailing and the weak. People started to leave as soon as they gained back enough strength for their journey. Slowly, the camp emptied out. Everyone wanted to go somewhere far from this dreadful place.

§ § § § §

Ede was drifting in and out of consciousness. Now, he was a handsome hussar prancing on his beautiful Arabian horse in the middle of Main Street in his hometown Kisvárda. His uniform made him even more of a handsome fellow than he normally was. The jacket of the tight, bright-blue hussar uniform was decorated with golden braids across his chest expatiated his wide shoulders. He was wearing red pants with long boots and he wore a tall hat on his head that was also decorated with golden braids, covering part of his high forehead and his full set of shiny black hair. Please do not forget to imagine the sword on his side. It was a bright sunny Sunday. Beautiful young ladies wearing their Sunday's best were strolling on the streets, all admiring him. They were all wearing beautiful long dresses and their freshly styled hair was covered with those cute little hats that were fashionable in those days. All of these ladies were using beautifully designed little fans to provide some relief from the hot summer air. These fans were also a good place to hide their blushing faces. He noticed that they were talking to each other, giggling, pointing, and smiling at him. He too was smiling and flirting with them. As usual, women loved him and he loved women. Suddenly, one of the most beautiful maiden runs over to him. When she gets close to him, she gently hit him with her fan and with a most beautiful smile and voice, she kept saying:

"Ede, Ede, Ede…" What was happening? The voice of the girl was getting deeper and deeper, and now the voice almost sounded like a man's voice. He opened his eyes and looked up…and the smiling face of his enormously large framed nurse appeared front of him.

"Ede please wake up already, it is time for you to take your medication." The nurse was handing him some pills and a glass of water.

Yes, he was back to reality, but what a reality! He was lying on a makeshift hospital bed in the Mauthausen camp. He and many of his fellow Jews became sick with typhus after the camp had been liberated. It took almost three month before Ede was able to start his journey back home. Home!? What home? By this time, he already knew that the Nazis had possibly killed millions of Jews. He suspected, rightfully, that most of his family had perished during the war due to the single-minded efforts of the "final solution" of the Nazis.

Many of the concentration camp survivors did not want to go back to their homes. They knew in their hearts that they would not be welcomed back by most of their non-Jewish neighbors. For many it was too painful even to think about starting over again, especially at home, where memories will forever remind them about their once happy past a past that was destroyed beyond repair. On the other hand, many returned home hoping to find some of their loved ones. Those who had gone home to find their family, but had returned only to have their hopes crushed moved on and pledged never to return.

Ede, as always, was full of hope and decided to restart his life in Hungary, for better or worse. By the end of June, Ede finally made it back to Kisvárda. In his father's house he found his youngest brother Arthur and the three sisters who had comeback with Helen. From Ede's large family of 10 brothers and sisters, only five survived. Their father was also killed.

"Ede," shouted Aranka his oldest sister, when she realized who was walking through the front door. "We were told that the Germans shot you after your failed escape."

They hugged, they cried, they laughed. It was a joyful reunion.

It is such a strange satisfying feeling to see any loved one who returned from almost certain death. This happiness was almost overshadowed by the pain of the loss of parents, sisters, brothers, cousins, friend, loved ones… Any news about a survivor brought an optimistic hope to find more friends and relatives who survived these horrible events. News of family members traveled with friend and relatives, but so many died, and many scattered all over the globe, they moved far away as possible from painful memories of the last few years. It happened quite often that family members did not know about the survival of each other and took many years to find each other. The memories of the Holocaust, death camps were hunting the survivors for the rest of their lives. They could never be completely happy; their happiness was ever marred by their past.

"Who told you that I was dead?" Ede asked.

"Your good friend Ármin." Ibi replied, his younger sister.

"He too survived?" Ede yelled he too believed that the Germans killed his friend.

"Yes, he was lucky." Aranka continued. "He was hiding in the farmer's barn where the Germans caught you. He spent three days in a barrel full of apples, being so small that the Germans did not find him. After the Germans left, he managed to cross over to the Russian side and came back to Kisvárda."

"Is there anyone else who survived from our family?" he asked. "Our father, our three brothers, and two sisters with their spouses and all their children have vanished."

"Yes, I assumed that since they are not here." Ede asked impatiently. "But who else whom we know came back?"

"Well, your wife Helen is at her parents' house in Nagydobos," Aranka said. "She was with us all through the camps and we all came back together."

"Why did not tell me this before!" He shouted. Ede's heart was pounding from excitement. His beloved wife was back, she had made it back! They had not seen each other for four long years. He could not wait any longer to see her.

Trains and busses were not yet running on a regular schedule, so he asked one of his neighbors to drive him with a horse drown carriage to Nagydobos. The two towns are not too far from each other, but in this difficult time, their trip took almost a day to complete. When he knocked at the door and Helen appeared at the doorway, they had a hard time recognizing each other. The beautiful young woman he left four years ago had become an old woman. She had the face of a person who suffered a great deal. The pain and suffering had carved deep furrows onto her face. Ede had lost a lot of weight; his face also showed the marks of suffering during the last few years, his posture was no longer straight and strong.

One can only imagine the joy of seeing again your loved one who you expected to be dead. Ede and Helen have made it and they are together again.

They hugged, they kissed, they cried from happiness. They could not let go of each other's hands and they stood embracing for so long that it seemed this would never end. Their love for each other followed them many years into the future. Their love helped them overcome the many problems they would encounter during the rest of their lives.

4

new life

Helen and Ede never had any children. Shortly after they married in 1939, Ede was drafted into the army's Force Labor Service and the couple had seen each other only a few times before they both were taken to various concentration camps. Having children in those unstable times was not a wise decision anyway. They were hoping that this madness would be over soon, and Helen and Ede would be able to start their family.

Many Jews returned to their old homes eager to find their family, many others never returned to Hungary. Some lucky families were able to reunite with some surviving loved ones. Unfortunately, many Jews found their homes empty and shortly after they arrived, decided to go somewhere far away. They wanted to settle in a place that was far enough to forget the past, to start a new life, a new beginning. Many immigrated to Palestine and swore they would never become vulnerable to the people who hate Jews. They swore never to allow becoming victims of anti-Semitism. The Jews who moved to Palestine wanted build a strong Jewish nation hoping that this Jewish nation would fight back those whose goal was to destroy the Jewish people never again permitting the world to create another Holocaust. Yet, many others went to countries like the USA, seeking out relatives who were willing help restart their broken lives. They went to the USA where religious freedom is written into its constitution.

§ § § § § §

The couple was uncertain about their future. They had a hard time deciding how to proceed in establishing their path to a new beginning. Like many others, Helen and Ede were unsure about their future, any future. Helen's health was fragile; she was weak. She would not be able to travel to such distant places like America. Her health situation helped to make their decision to stay in Hungary. Ede's hope to go to America had to wait for many years to come. For a while, they remained in Helen's parents' house in Nagydobos along with Icú. In early summer of 1946, Icú got married and left for Palestine. Nagydobos was a tiny agricultural village in the northeast of Hungary. There was little opportunity for Ede to find any suitable job in this tiny village. Ede did not know nor did he have any desire to learn either farming or any work related to farming. He was a well-educated man; he was not destined to perform physical labor. Unfortunately, they did not have enough money to start a new business venture as an alternative.

It was six o'clock in the morning and the sun had already made its present known, the air in the bedroom was getting warm. He sat up in his bed and looked out the open window. The bright sunshine promised that today will be just one more hot lazy summer day. The calendar showed 1946. Ede had been home with Helen for almost a year. During this time, he started to look like his old self again. Ede became restless and frustrated. His job situation remained unresolved. At the spur of a moment, he got up, got dressed, and told Helen he was going to Budapest. He caught the early morning train to Budapest with a hope to find some of his old friends. Before the war, Ede was active in politics and he had been a member of the Smallholders Party. After the war, the Smallholders Party took a leading role in the political scene in Hungary's government.

§ § § § § §

In December 1944, a temporary Hungarian government was formed. A multi-party political system was started under the watchful eyes of the Soviet authorities. On January 20, 1945, the Hungarian peace treaty was signed in Moscow. By the summer of 1946, a new Hungarian government introduced a new currency, the Forint, and tried to stabilize the political and economical environment in Hungary and tried to stop the highest inflation-rate in the history of the world. People got paid twice a day to soften the effect of the three-digit daily inflation rate. This new government made efforts to create a true democratic form of government, but could not shake off the Soviet influences completely. The occupying forces of the Soviet Union filled the gap left by the defeated German army and the Soviets were in complete control of Hungary. In the beginning, worrying about world opinion, the Soviets allowed the Hungarians to form a democratic government.

Under the influence of Soviet Union, a strong Communist Party was organized and its members were trained to take over the control of the Hungarian government. Before the war, many Hungarian Communists were hiding in the Soviet Union from the right-wing Hungarian authorities. The Soviet Union sent these Communists along with many newly recruited and brainwashed prisoners of war to Hungary and started to make the transformation to convert Hungary to a Communist state. The Hungarian communists collaborated with the Soviets and made every effort to legislate new laws without popular consent. After the first general election, the people of Hungary overwhelmingly elected the coalition of non-communists parties, and the Small Holders Party gained control of the central government. The coalition of all independent parties worked hard to keep the Communists away from controlling the country. This strategy did work for a while.

For the surviving Jewish population, these years were relatively peaceful. Like the rest of the population, they too were struggling to make a decent living. Jews felt much safer than they had for many years in the past. Many Jews joined all kinds of governmental agencies. Their motivation was for years to come to seek out all the war criminals of the Hungarian Arrow Cross (Nazi) Party and indict them, one-way or another. This motivation was the primary reason for many Jews to join the Secret Service (ÁVH—Államvédelmi Hatóság) of the Communists. Inside this organization, they were able to attain, many times unlimited, authority and they were able to eliminate some of these despicable human trash legally or otherwise.

§ § § § § §

Arthur, Ede's brother, also joined the local Communist party hoping that their leftist ideology and the backing of the Soviets would help his fellow Jews become an integral part of the emerging new society. Of course, the sound of comrade Kupferstein (elvtárs in Hungarian) did not resonate well. He changed his last name to a more typical Hungarian name: Kádár. The people who changed their names to a Hungarian sounding name would usually change their name to a name that started with the same initials as the old one. This was how the name Kádár was chosen by Arthur. Ede did not approve of the change, but he decided to go along with it because he had only one surviving brother and it would not feel right for two bothers to have two different last names. Ede also applied for the name change.

§ § § § § §

By the time Ede arrived in Budapest, government agencies had already appointed people to most of their political positions, and only a few important jobs remained unfilled. Ede arrived at the Eastern Railroad Station (Keleti Pályaudvar) in Budapest. The devastating effects of the war were still highly visible. The Battle of Budapest was one of the bloodiest, devastating sieges of World War II. The beautiful city of Budapest was in ruins, with more than 80 percent of its buildings either destroyed or damaged. Historical buildings like the Hungarian Parliament Building and the Kings Palace on Buda hills were badly damaged. All five bridges spanning the Danube were destroyed by the withdrawing German troops.

By this time, the war in Hungary had been over for more than a year. The streets were jam-packed with all kinds of carts, horse drawn carriages, and trucks. Everyone was carrying whatever rummages he or she was able to remove and clean up from collapsed and damaged buildings. People were working mostly with their bare hands to tear down partially collapsed buildings. Most of the broken rails for the trams had not yet been repaired. Only a few tramlines were running and only a limited numbers of busses were available for public transportations. Rubble was covering parts of the broken sidewalks and roads. Clearing the streets was the first step to try to restore normal life for the people of Budapest and to give them some work until factories and other industries could start operating again. Ede had to walk to everywhere.

Ede visited several people, Jewish and non-Jewish friends, and acquaintances. One of his good friends informed Ede that their old campaign buddy, Zoltán Tildy, was the head of the Smallholders Party and had secured himself a high government job (later he became the president of the Hungarian Republic). Ede immediately went to see him. He was lucky, Zoltán was in his office, and he welcomed Ede. Ede had a great personality combined with being a well-spoken, smooth conversationalist. He was able to achieve almost anything he wanted. He had the reputation as a "good salesman." People who knew Ede well, always referred to him as a man who could sell refrigerators to the Eskimos at the North Pole. As expected, he succeeded. Zoltán appointed Ede as the Director of Displaced Properties for three counties in the southeast of Hungary starting August 1,

1946. Ede, as a newly mandated government official, became responsible for helping displaced Jewish families who had returned from concentration camps get back their own properties and other valuables that were taken by their gentile neighbors after all the Jews had been taken away by the Nazis. The only problem with this new job was that he had to move to either Békéscsaba or Gyula, which were over 250 kilometers away from Nagydobos.

Hearing the news, Helen was not too thrilled about moving so far away to an unfamiliar city, but at this point, they did not have many options. Ede explained to his wife that this job would be a good job. Ede felt that since he had been given this opportunity to help his fellow Jews, he had no choice but to fulfill his new responsibility with enthusiasm.

§ § § § § §

Before the war, over three thousand Jews were living in Békéscsaba. Jewish communities were well organized all around the country. They kept careful, up to date listings of all members of the Jewish community, the community members religious affiliation was not important as long as they were Jewish. All Jews were important to any Jewish community. If someone needed help, help from the community was always available. Unfortunately, this practice also helped the local anti-Semites point out Jews to the authorities. The mass deportations of Jews started not long after German forces occupied Hungary on March 19, 1944. Between July 24 and July 26, 1944, most Jews in Békéscsaba were rounded up and shipped to Auschwitz. Many local gentiles seized this opportunity to take everything from the evacuated Jewish homes. Some just moved right into the vacated house and the local authorities did not care nor do anything against this practice. Authorities closed their eyes to these actions and secretly, and sometimes openly also grabbed the opportunity to obtain Jewish valuables left by their owners. These despicable people justified their actions by declaring that Jews would never return. Thank G-d they were wrong. A relatively large number of Jews, approximately five hundred, survived the war and returned to their homes in Békéscsaba.

Ede had a choice to open his office either in Gyula, the current county seat of Békés County, a smaller, very pleasant city located nearby Békéscsaba or in Békéscsaba a relatively large city with a larger Jewish population than Gyula. A few days later, Ede was ready to inspect Békéscsaba and Gyula, their future residence for the next few years. He wanted to check out the city of Gyula also, but first he went to Békéscsaba. His first task was to find a suitable house where they could move in as soon as possible. He was looking for a larger house where he could set up his residence with his wife and have enough space for an office. On his trip, he also wanted to get a glimpse of the local population so he could get an expectation for their new life in this strange city. A new life in a city, in a city where they did not know a single sole, would not be easy. This was the first time Ede visited Békéscsaba and this part of Hungary. For Ede to belong in a strong Jewish community was very important.

Ede was an observant Jew. In Hungary, his kind of religious affiliation was defined as Orthodox. The obvious first place he would visit was the local Jewish community. He was very interested in what kind of Jewish life still existed in this city. He was pleasantly surprised to find a considerable Jewish community, which was in the process of organizing itself. He met some of the leaders of the congregation including their newly elected president, Mr. Moskowics. Ede presented his credentials and gave the details and responsibilities of his new job. They were very happy to see him and welcomed Ede into their community. Someone recommended an abandoned beautiful villa located not far from the center of the city and suggested that it could be well suited for his purpose. The house had been damaged during the war, but was not beyond repair. The original Jewish owners probably perished during the Holocaust.

The villa on 3 Trefort Street was built in the early 1930s. It was constructed to be an extremely luxurious house for its time. When this villa was built, most houses in Békéscsaba had no indoor plumbing. Unlike all the other houses on the same street, this house was much taller with large windows, suggesting bright rooms with high ceilings. A beautiful stone and iron fence separated the house from the street. Between the house and the fence was a garden for flowers. On the right side of the house, a stone garden could be found with the remnants of exotic flowers. To the left of the house, between the villa and the neighbor's house, a large iron gate allowed vehicles into the property and a wide roadway led into the backyard. A long utility building was located at the end of this roadway. The building contained an apartment for the house servants, a stable where in the past horses were kept, a couple of storage rooms for firewood and coal for winter heating and an outhouse that was probably used by the housekeeping personnel. The apartment was small, with one large room and a kitchen. One could imagine that the backyard used to be covered with grass and flowerbeds, but the years of neglect had destroyed everything. A manual water pump was used to pump non-drinking water from the well for general use. An electric water pump was used to supply drinking water to the main house. The drinking water was first pumped into a large cement tank located on the attic and a set of pipes linked to the kitchen, bathroom, laundry room and the toilets. Along the entire right side of the property there was a four-meter high solid brick fence providing complete privacy from the neighbors. Between this fence and the house, a narrow triangular area was used to keep chickens and other farm animals before they were slaughtered for consumption. This area also housed the underground septic tank, since no public utilities existed in this area of the town.

The villa was built to be one of most elegant houses in Békéscsaba. Up to one meter pedestal of the main building was made of quarry stone. Above the stones, the beige plastered walls were broken up only by large windows. The tall steeped roof was made of red clay roofing tiles. The sidewalk leading from the street along the building was made of yellow ceramic tiles that looked exceptionally decorative, but during the winter, it could become so slippery that one had to be careful not to fall on it. Under an archway, ten marble steps led to the main entrance of the house. A double entrance door opened into a small attractive hallway. From this hallway, there were several doors led to various rooms of the house. The entrance hall led to two small rooms, one with a joining toilet. A beautiful wooden door with stained glass windows led into the large entertainment room. This large room spanned the full length of the house. Two marble columns, shiny parquet floors and beautifully designed plastered ceilings and walls made this room elegant. On one end, there was a podium with a French door leading to an attractive terrace. The floor of the terrace was covered by Italian marble. The terrace was surrounded by carved stonewall with flowerpots on top. The entertainment room was divided by a wall-to-wall French door. This door could be completely folded up so the two separate rooms could be used as one large ballroom or for any other entertainment purposes. In total, the villa had six rooms, two toilets, and a bathroom with running water coming from its own well, a kitchen, a large pantry, and a utility room. It was a very large house even by today's standards.

Ede liked the house and decided to obtain it. The villa needed a great deal of repairs and he knew that the Budapest office would not finance the cost of repair for this elaborate house.

After Ede returned to Nagydobos, they sold Helen's parent's house and spent most of the proceeds to renovate and furnish the villa in Békéscsaba. By late summer of 1946, all repairs were complete.

However, the authorities were dragging their feet in granting the occupancy permit. The move to Békéscsaba was delayed again and again. The house was too big for only two people. The combined living area of six rooms and utility rooms was much larger than most people would need in Békéscsaba and probably bigger than most homes in Hungary. After the war, families became homeless and were living in very tight quarters. People would love the opportunity to live in this house. The most likely reason Ede had tremendous problems obtaining the occupancy permit was the fact that other families were badly in need of decent housing. Finally, the central committee of the Displaced Properties in Budapest applied some pressure to the local authorities in Békéscsaba, the permit was issued on November 11, 1946, and the Kádár family was ready to move in.

§ § § § § §

In late November of 1946, Helen and Ede moved all their belongings to Békéscsaba. The two smaller rooms near the main entrance and one of the bathrooms became the office of the Director of Displaced Properties. A large sign was put up in the front of the building making it official: the office of the Director of Displaced Properties was open for business. The rest of the house served as their residence. The entry door from the terrace became the entrance to the home of Ede and Helen. The main entrance hall served as the access to Ede's office. This way, receiving clients would not interfere with their home life. The couple brought all their furniture from Nagydobos, but because the house was very big, some rooms were left completely empty for many years to come and the Kádár family never used those rooms.

§ § § § § §

A large segment of Békéscsaba residents were descendants of northern Slavs. These people were commonly identified as Tótok. In the seventeenth century, the occupying Turks were defeated by the Habsburgs and left Hungary forever. Slavic populations from the north were encouraged by the local government to move into Békés County to repopulate this devastated area. The land was, and still is, very fertile. The new landowners needed people to work on these fields. The newcomers kept their heritage and their language over the centuries. After WWII was over, these locals, for some reason, felt that the time had come to move away from the Hungarian culture and to readapt their own culture again. They seemed to resent the Hungarians even though they were living among them for centuries.

To be removed from one's familiar surroundings, always been hard for everyone. For Helen, the transition to the new life in Békéscsaba was hard. At the stores and the flea markets, Helen had a hard time communicating with the locals of Slavic heritage. They refused to talk to Helen in Hungarian. Even though everyone spoke Hungarian, the Tótok would rarely answer back to her in Hungarian; obviously some of these people did not welcome her in her new neighborhood.

§ § § § § §

Both Helen and Ede were observant Jews and their religious background brought them closer to the local Jewish community that welcomed them with open arms. In no time, they made new friends and they felt right at home in the Jewish community.

Many Jews who came back from the concentration camps were not able to take possessions of their own houses and other properties they had left behind when the German Nazis deported them. Ede searched out all resettling Jews and tried to help them the best he could. His job to help repatriate his fellow Jews was very gratifying. He kept careful listings of each items, including their current value, the recipient, and the "donor's" names. Ede strongly believed that his new work was given to him by G-d and it had become his destiny. He enjoyed his power tremendously. He, a Jew who had been humiliated and looked down upon by the bottom of the Hungarian society, could now pay back the "favor" and could humiliate these vile people without any consequence to himself. He was on the top and they were on the bottom. If any Jew declared a particular property as his, Ede would transfer that item to them even if Ede suspected that these items had never been owned by the claimant. Because of his authority, the gentiles who currently owned these items could do absolutely nothing about Ede's decisions!

Ede always used the local police to remove all claimed items from the current "owners." He also had a gun-permit so just in case he ran into any trouble with taking possession of goods he could defend himself. He never had any problems and never had a reason to fire his gun. His office in the villa was open for business day and night. The Jewish communities were happy to see him and his dedication. He had all the support and help from the local authorities and from the honest people around him. He became a well-known and well-respected official in the area.

§ § § § § §

The Hungarian Jews were organized into three distinct religious hierarchies: Orthodox, Neology and Statusquo ante. Before the war, each division was managed by separate national organizations. In cities and villages, small and large, throughout Hungary, all three branches were represented.

The orthodoxy followed more traditional Jewish laws and ethics of the Talmud. In addition to the laws and ethics of the Talmud, it also contains rabbinical discussions and interpretations of Jewish laws and ethics. The Hassidic movement, whose members were mostly living in small villages in Hungary, was considered part of the Orthodoxy. In most cases, the Rabbi's sermon was delivered in Yiddish the traditional language spoken by European Jews.

The Neology movement came from a reform movement within the Hungarian speaking regions of Europe beginning in the 19th century. The reforms that the Neology movement installed were comparable to the more traditional wing of the US Conservative Judaism. Women and men were seated in separate areas. Even though the prayer services were conducted mostly in Hebrew, the Rabbi's sermon was delivered in Hungarian. Some synagogues employed a non-Jewish organ player enhance the pleasure of listening to the singing of the choir. Sometimes the choir included women also.

The Statusquo ante movement had taken position between the two other movements. They were just as religious as the Orthodoxy, but in the Statusquo ante synagogues, the Rabbis used the Hungarian language instead of the traditional Yiddish, and their members were observant Jews.

As the Communists gained more and more power, they meddled with every aspect of people's lives. The Communists started to limit religious freedom and put restrictions on how religious organizations could function. The government allowed only one Jewish hierarchy and forced the Orthodox and Neology into a single organizational structure, albeit with a semi-autonomous Orthodox section. The Statusquo ante hierarchy completely disappeared. The Jewish leadership in Budapest assigned local Rabbis to most Jewish communities without any regards to the local community's needs. Existing Rabbis were accepted and stayed in their positions.

There was no acting Rabbi in Békéscsaba. Ede, as a religious Jew, was afraid that his newly adopted community would end up with a Neology Rabbi. He organized a meeting with the leaders of the Jewish community of Békéscsaba to devise a plan to assure that the community will be Orthodox, even though he knew that the majority of the Jews in Békéscsaba were not interested keeping kosher or being religious at all.

"As a 'Shomer Shabbat' (Shabbat observer) Jew like many of you, we must decide what kind of Jewish community we want." Ede started to address the people gathered. "In the past, I always belonged to an Orthodox community. I want to continue my tradition. Isn't this what you all want?"

"As you all know, we do not have a Rabbi. We need an Orthodox Rabbi who will lead us, to define us as an Orthodox community," said Mr. Moskowics, the president.

"We cannot wait until Budapest appoints a Rabbi. They could send us either a Neology or an Orthodox Rabbi," said the Shamash, Uncle Yayli, the community's caretaker, a Hassidic Jew.

Mr. Neiman was the religion teacher of the community, a shochet, (ritual slaughter) and he had all the qualifications to become their Rabbi. He was also a Hassidic Jew. However, he did not want to accept the big responsibility of becoming the leader of the community. Even before this meeting, the community leaders tried to convince him to be their Rabbi, but he refused the offer.

"Could any of you recommend somebody who might be suitable for this job?" Ede was pressing.

"I heard about a Hassidic Jew, a teacher in Püspökladány. He is a Talmud chacham (scholar), shochet, well qualified for the job. He might take this job," one of the congregant suggested.

"We need to investigate this possibility," Mr. Moskowics concluded. "Let us send someone over to Püspökladány as soon as possible and let us try to convince him to take this job. Let us hope he is willing to do it."

"Who should go?" There were differing opinions about what to do next.

"Even if this person took the job, the Budapest central committee might not approve our decision," some attendants were questioning the plan with concerned voices.

"They have to accept our decision, especially if we elect a new Rabbi as soon as possible. By the time they wake up, it would be too late to change. We already have a Rabbi and the case is closed," suggested Ede.

"We will let the central committee know about our decision only after the Rabbi already settled in Békéscsaba." Mr. Moskowics endorsed the plan. It was a sneaky move. Everyone liked it and concession was agreed.

"Let us not waste any more time," the president recommended. "I want Ede and Mr. Neiman to visit Mr. Schnitzler tomorrow."

The next day, the two delegates boarded the train to Püspökladány. They did not even know Mr. Shnitzler's address, but Püspökladány was a small town and they were sure they would find Mr. Schnitzler. Typically, in small town Hungary the local synagogues were located somewhere in the center of the town.

Ede and Mr. Neiman got off the train and headed toward the center of the town. After a short walk, they spotted the synagogue gracefully standing near the center square of the town. They assumed that Mr. Schnitzler must live nearby.

"Shalom Aleichem" Ede and Mr. Neiman greeted the man opening the door of the house located next to the Synagogue. To spot the right house was easily due to the Jewish custom of having a mezuzah affixed to the doorframe.

"Shalom Aleichem," Mr. Schnitzler greeted the strangers. He was tall, his long black well-maintained beard covering most of his chest. His payes (sideburns) were neatly curled and freely hanging from behind his ears. His eyes were bright suggesting a smart, kind person. He was wearing a long black jacket coming down almost to his knees with a white shirt underneath the jacket. This statuesque man overshadowed the two delegates, not in a frightening way, but some kind of saintly manner.

"What can I do for you?" Mr. Schnitzler continued with a slightly shy smile on his face, inviting the two men into his house.

"Well, we are in an interesting, trying circumstance." Mr. Neiman started.

"We come from Békéscsaba and our mission is to find an Orthodox Rabbi for our community," he continued.

The shy smile of Mr. Schnitzler face was morphed into a surprised expression. He wondered why these strangers were informing him about this important search. He was a simple man of G-d. He had no desire to take on such a big responsibly of being a Rabbi. Nevertheless, he was listening. He was sure these people came for his advice.

The delegates explained to him their dilemma.

"We made a choice to appoint an orthodox Rabbi instead of waiting for the decision to come from Budapest. The Jewish community of Békéscsaba might end up with someone with lesser qualifications than you have." Ede made clear their intention. "The Jewish population in Békéscsaba is much larger and we have a small contingent of Hassidic Jews like you. For your family, Békéscsaba would be a much better place to live than this small village of Püspökladány, where only a handful of Jews remain."

"We have a nice house that had been used by a long list Rabbis before the war where you can move in with your family as soon as you wish. This house is large enough for your five children." Mr. Neiman concluded the offer.

"I have to discuss the offer with my wife," Mr. Schnitzler responded. "I will notify you of my decision shortly." A few days later, Mr. Moskowics received a telegram from Mr. Schnitzler accepting the Rabbi position. He also requested guidance about his move into the promised house in Békéscsaba. The issue of the position of Rabbi was solved.

§ § § § § §

It is interesting that newspapers and radio news bulletins inform people about news from around the world or about local communities. However, the spread of "real news" is best achieved by word of mouth, or another way of saying via the local rumor-mill. You hear one story, and then you hear another story from someone else. It is funny, but true, the two stories might be about the same thing putting on a different twist. Ede heard these stories, rumors about a Jewish boy living with a gentile family in Békés, a village not far from Békéscsaba. The rumors also mentioned a lawyer named Dr. Pintér. He had to investigate this rumor since it involved a Jewish boy. As with any other rumors, Ede needed to act quickly. In the past, when for some reason or another, he had hesitated to act upon and delayed to investigate, the items in question quickly disappeared, and Ede was not able to complete his job.

Ede took the train to Békés a smaller village about 10 kilometers away. Békéscsaba and Békés were connected by a narrow-gage rail line. A small, almost toy like steam engine was pulling a few wagons, passengers, and cargo. One of the interesting things about this train was its itinerary. The train started from the main railroad station in Békéscsaba and led through the main street of the city, passing through the center of the town. The train would make several stops within the city limits before it left for Békés. It was a slow train. Normally, the ride took almost an hour to get into Békés. The train ride took this long not only because the train was moving very slowly, but also because the train made many stops before reaching its destination, Békés.

Ede's first stop was at the local police station, where he was already well known. He went directly to see the police chief.

"Good morning, Józsi," Ede greeted him.

"Good morning," he replied, "what brings you here today?"

By now, the police chief already knew that whenever Ede visited him it was always somehow connected to Jews. He did not like these visits, nor did he like the idea of cooperating with Ede or any other Jews. Ede had the authority, and like many other government organizations, Józsi had no choice but to cooperate to the fullest, before he would get himself into any trouble. Józsi was no friends of Jews! He was a police officer in Békés before, during, and after the war.

In mid-May 1944, the Hungarian authorities along with the local police force, where Józsi was working at the time, helped the Nazis to seek out and deport the local Jewish population. After the war was over, he rejoined the police force again and claimed that, as many had done "he had no choice" but to cooperate with the Germans. The local government of Békés had already been infiltrated with Communists and Communist sympathizers. An experienced policeman with a less than perfect conscience was perfect for their plans. He claimed again, he had no choice...

"Do you know Dr. Pintér, the lawyer?" Ede asked.

"Sure," he replied quickly. "Hej, Jancsi, go get Dr. Pintér," he yelled to his deputy. Before Ede even could protest, the deputy left in a hurry and a few minutes later, he was back with the lawyer.

Dr. Pintér was scared. We should not be surprised that he was scared. In those days, when the police showed up at your doorstep unannounced it was bad news for you. One did not need to be guilty in order to get arrested for a crime that was completely unknown to the person who was arrested.

"Good morning Dr. Pintér." Ede tried to calm him down. Ede knew how Dr. Pintér was feeling. He saw how the Communists detained many innocent citizens who might not have the same enthusiasm about building the Communist "wonderland."

"I need to talk with you about the Jewish boy. Let us go to your house, where we could talk more freely," continued Ede. They left the police station and headed toward his house. Dr. Pintér's house was on a serene street where behind tall oak trees, small one-family houses were hiding. This area of the town was pleasant and located in a quiet neighborhood of Békés. Dr. Pintér had a well-kept little house with a big backyard. The backyard was separated by a tall fence revealing a garden filled with vegetable plants and fruit trees on one side toward the back of the house. A cozy shaded flower garden with chairs and tables was located closer to the main entrance. After they went into the house, they sat down in Dr. Pintér's office, a small room with a beautiful antique desk facing the door and a few shelves full of books. By now, Dr. Pintér seemed to have calmed down, realizing that he was not in trouble after all.

"So, tell me all you know about this boy." Ede encouraged the lawyer to talk. Dr. Pintér told the story. He explained how Mr. Hajdú found the baby at the railroad yard in an empty wagon and took him home. He praised the couple for bringing the orphan into their house with love. He described his appreciation for the way the Hajdú family was taking care of Lacika just life he were their own child.

"It is very nice to hear this, but are you sure that this child is Jewish?" Ede impatiently asked the lawyer.

"I strongly believe that the boy is Jewish, since he was circumcised as Jewish boys usually are."

"I do not believe that any Jewish boy should be raised by a Christian family," Ede continued, "I want to find the legal way to place this Jewish boy with a suitable Jewish family." Ede told the lawyer to look into this matter and report to him about the progress. The lawyer assured Ede that he would help to find the legal way of placing the boy into a Jewish family once Ede found a suitable family.

After Ede left the lawyer's house, he immediately went back to the police station to talk to the police chief again.

"Józsi, do you have any documentation about this boy who was found at the railroad station in Földvár in 1945?"

"I believe we do" he replied, "let me find it for you." Józsi went to another office and returned shortly with a couple of hand written pieces of paper with several signatures. These documents were testimonies of the police chief from Földvár and other witnesses describing the circumstances of finding the baby in mid-October 1945. Ede took these documents and headed to the railroad station to return home to Békéscsaba.

It was past lunchtime by the time Ede got home. As usual, his wife, Helen, was impatiently waiting for her husband with a hot lunch she

Nyilatkozat.

Alulírott Farkas János Békés-földvári lakos aki 1945. évben, az Államrendőrség helybeli önparancsnoka voltam, a következőkben adom elő, nyilatkozatomat, Hivatalos helységünk a Békés-földvári, állomás épületében volt elhelyezve. Különös gondot fordítottam arra, hogy az Állomásra érkező, és ki-induló vonat szerelvényeket alapossággal átvizsgáljam.

1945. okt. közepén egy ilyen szerelvény átvizsgálatok alkalmával, egy üres vasúti teherkocsiban egy gyereket találtam, a gyereket kivéve a kocsiból megállapíttottam, hogy a gyerek egy jól fejlett, egészséges színű kis fiúcska volt, ami úgy az én mint több jelenlevő véleménye szerint 1 éves lehetet. Mint rendőrember nyomozás eredménye ként meg állapíttottam, hogy a szerelvény, az állomáson átjött annak mozdonya, szerelvény nélkül Békés-csabára ment be, és az Budapest, illetve Szolnok felől jött. megállapíttottuk hogy míg az üres szerelvény a B-földvári állomáson tartózkodott, addig szabadságolt katonákat hozó szerelvények mentek keresztül és tartottak pihenőt, és így egész biztos hogy a Theodor Ede által később örökbe fogadott fent leírt körülmények között talált kis fiúcska.

WITNESS DECLARATION—FINDING A CHILD IN OCTOBER 1945

prepared earlier that morning. The lives of most people was still affected by the destruction and shortages caused by the war. Rationing by the government was introduced for basic food items like bread, sugar, butter, and meat to try to minimize the effect of food shortage on the general population. However, ever since her husband had gotten his high government post, most of the food rationing that others had to endure had little effect on the Kádár family. Besides, when Helen needed anything that happened to be missing at the government-managed stores, Helen was able to buy it "freely" on the black market. The cost of goods brought on the black market was forbiddingly high for most others, but Ede was paid very well and the extra cost did not affect their lifestyle at all.

§ § § § § §

The couple sat down to eat. First, they ate the soup without which a Hungarian lunch would not be complete. This time, it was a summer vegetable soup with homemade noodles (nokedli), one of Ede's favorite soups.

"Guess what I was doing today?" Ede coyly said to Helen.

"I haven't the faintest," was the quick reply. "Probably you gave a sewing machine to one of the Jews in Békés who does not even know how to use a sewing machine." Ede was known to have a soft spot for helping any Jew who were asking for help. Ede would do almost anything for a needy Jew; he would not rest until he could fulfill the request using all of his power and influence.

"Well, my darling, this time you are wrong," Ede said with a smile.

"It was hard to believe that I did not guess your actions," Helen answered with a wide smile on her face.

"I have found a son for you."

"What are you talking about?" Helen was trying to make a serious face and fighting her urge to break up laughing.

"Yes, you heard well. I found a SON for us!"

"How can you just find a son? They aren't just lying around somewhere to be found."

Ever since Helen came back from Auschwitz, her health never recovered to the way it was before the war. She was constantly in pain and discomfort due to the poor health caused by the conditions at the concentration camps. She was full of pains, "female" problems she always complained about, and G-d knows what else was wrong with her. She never discussed her problems with anyone. Even if she tried to have a baby of her own, she could not. While she was in the concentration camp, they had performed some kind of operation on her because she developed an infection in her uterus. Under these circumstances, she could not even think to have a child of her own. Besides by now, Helen was over 40 years old, she would not want the complications of a pregnancy at this age. Even though she badly wanted a child, they had never considered adopting one. Finding Lacika played into their wishes of finally having a little one running around.

It was an easy decision. They agreed to adopt this orphan no matter what it took to get him. Even though Ede had a lot of power, adoption cases were not among his responsibilities, nor did he have the authority to make it happen. He had no jurisdiction dealing with children, only dealing with property. Ede knew they would have an uphill battle to adopt this child, but we know that for Ede nothing was impossible. Ede did not to waste any time taking Lacika into his house. He did not want to wait for some bureaucrat to dismiss his claim for Lacika. As he had always done, he took care of business his own way.

5

the adoption

The tears were dripping down on her face. She felt like part of her life was being torn away from her.

"I cannot believe this, how could anyone do this to me?" She was crying uncontrollably. "I raised this wonderful child as my own. I am the one who spent sleepless nights watching over him when he was sick." She could not stop crying. Yes, for Eszti, it was extremely unfair that Lacika was being taken away from her.

On February 16, 1947, a large black automobile stopped in the front of the house of the Hajdú family. A policeman stepped out and knocked on the door. Eszti wiped away her tears and opened the door with dread knowing the inevitable: Lacika would be taken away from her for good. A few days ago, the Hajdú family was notified that Mr. Ede Kádár, the Director of Displaced Properties, would be taking Lacika away, but Eszti and János were hoping that this day would never come. A couple of months ago Dr. Pintér, the lawyer came over and told Eszti that Mr. Kádár had filed a petition to take Lacika away from her. Ever since, she knew this event would come but Eszti tried to block it out from her mind. She was not able to do so, but she and her husband were still hoping. They had filed an appeal to keep Lacika, but nothing happened, not even an acknowledgement of receipt of the petition.

The day finally arrived. The policeman showed her an official looking document that demanded that a three years old child named László Földvári must be handed over to him. A man and a woman got out from the automobile and approached her.

"My name is Ede Kádár and this is my wife Helen." the man said. "We are sorry about this, but we feel this is the right thing to do for Lacika."

"You may come to see Lacika any time you want," the woman continued. "I do understand why you are so upset. I promise you that he will be loved and will be well taken care of for the rest of his life."

The woman picked up the little child, who looked confused. Helen hugged him, kissed him and for the first time in her life, her motherly instinct took over her frame of mind. "I am a mother," she told herself and tears of happiness formed in the corner of her eyes. Eszti had not expected these people to be kind and respectful; she somehow pictured Ede and Helen as some kind of stuck-up insolent people. "I was probably wrong, these people seem to be nice," she told herself and quickly turned around and shut the door, before anyone would see the tears running down her face.

§ § § § §

Shortly after, Ede had visited Dr Pintér and he submitted an application to the Bureau of Orphan's Welfare to request for the adoption of Lacika. Neither Ede nor Helen had seen the child yet, but they determined to adopt him nevertheless. The adoption of any war orphans was a relatively simple procedure. Authorities performed a cursory background check and if no criminal records were discovered about the people trying to adopt, the child was given to the applicant in a manner of days. The government was happy when someone was willing to lessen the burden of taking care of hundreds and thousands of these orphans. In the case of Lacika however, the adoption process was much more complicated. He lived with a reputable foster family and the family did not want to give him up. The government did not care if the family was poor or rich as long as the child was out of their hands. The Government bureaucrats did not care about the religious differences between the child and his adaptive family. For some reason bureaucracy was working at its best. For a long time nothing was done to expedite the adoption process of Lacika.

Eszti tried her hardest to keep Lacika. She sent a petition to the Displaced Properties ministry in Budapest as soon she discovered Ede's intentions. She did not even receive a reply from them. She could not even find out what had happened to her letter.

In the meantime, Ede received a letter from the deputy minister of the Displaced Properties ministry. The deputy sent a letter to Ede to report to him about why did Ede was trying to take the Jewish boy away from the Hajdú family. Ede should know that this kind of matter was not within his jurisdiction. Ede was the official responsible in this area of the country for lost and displaced properties, but a child is not considered property according to the bureaucrats in Budapest. The only reason the deputy was acting in this matter was because they received the petition from Eszti. The central office did not want to get involved with a small item like this, but they wanted to be informed of the progress of this issue. The letter was originally sent to Békés (instead of Ede Kádár Elek Kádár was the addressee) so by the time Ede received this mail, the adoption was already approved. Besides, Ede would not do anything about the request that would jeopardize his own plans. Why should he? He wanted to adopt the child and that was it.

§ § § § § §

Dr. Pintér was not sure which side to support in the adoption of Lacika. He was well aware that the Hajdú family was doing a wonderful job raising this child, but underneath he also understood that this child was Jewish, a victim of circumstances during the uncertain times that followed the Great War. He also realized that the Jews, who had survived the concentration camps, have a strong determination to rebuild their lives and embrace everyone who could be considered a part of their greater family. Every soul that could be saved would make the Jewish community that much stronger. He also suspected that Lacika would have a much better future with a well-educated, high social standing middle class family compared to the limited opportunities that the Hajdú family would be able to provide for Lacika.

Dr. Pintér decided to intervene in this affair; after all, he was the official guardian of the child. He went to Békéscsaba to talk it over with Ede. He knew where Ede's office was and he walked into the office without any hesitation. In the office, he found only the secretary, a young, tall, gorgeous blond woman.

"Good morning," he greeted her.

"Good morning," the girl answered with a lovely voice and a big smile on her pretty face, "what can I do for you?" The unexpected encounter with this attractive woman distracted Dr. Pintér for a minute. He was not young anymore but he could still be attracted to a beauty like this. "Hmm, what could she help me with...?" He wondered for a minute. It seemed for a moment that he completely forgot the reason for coming into the office. We all know that Ede was a "ladies man" and he would not hire an old ugly woman for his secretary. Besides she had lots of talents...among them, she knew how to type and truly, she did not make too many typos. Helen was not so thrilled having a "talented" woman around Ede and she did not appreciate the flirting what went on inside his office. This alleged flirting could have only been in Helen's imagination, but knowing Ede's reputation... (who knows?)

"My name is Dr. Pintér, an attorney, I have come to see Mr. Kádár," he finally snapped into reality, chasing away his "dirty" thoughts.

"Is he expecting you?" she asked him with a pleasant voice that made Dr. Pintér uncomfortable again. "I should not think of that now, I have a different, more important purpose for my visit!" he kept telling himself, but he was still eyeing the girl.

"No, he does not know I was coming."

"I am sorry, but Mr. Kádár is not in the office and I do not know when he will return." Dr. Pintér realized that he should have called the office to make an appointment with Mr. Kádár to assure that he would not waste his time coming to an empty office. He knew that Mr. Kádár was always very busy and it was somewhat foolish to expect that Ede would be in his office at all times.

"Is Mrs. Kádár home?" he asked the secretary.

"I believe so," she replied. "But, she does not get involved with any official business of the Displaced Properties office."

"Well," he said, "the reason for my visit involves her too."

"Please go around in the back of the house and you will find a terrace leading to the entrance into their residence," she instructed him.

"Thank you Miss. Goodbye." Dr. Pintér was still mesmerized by the beauty of the secretary. While he tried to leave, he had a hard time finding the door and almost tumbled over a chair standing nearby. The secretary was smiling at the all too familiar scene, that she had seen many times in the office when young and old men came to visit. He walked around the building into the backyard, not realizing that more surprises were still waiting him.

He rang the entrance bell and Helen opened the door. They had never met, so Helen had no idea who this distinguished looking gentleman was.

§ § § § §

More than three years had passed since she returned from the concentration camps. She had gained some weight during this time and honestly, she may even have put on a little bit too much. Even though she was troubled with poor health, one could not guess by looking at her. Her health troubles were totally invisible to people who did not know her issues. She was 41 years old, but she looked younger than her age and again, she looked very attractive. Her life had finally become stable and now she had the easiest time of her life ever with the exception of when she was a very young girl at her parents' house. Helen was in the middle of cooking lunch and wearing her home gown with a colorful apron tied around her waist. As usual, her head was covered with a scarf, the way most orthodox married Jewish woman should. She was not expecting any visitors at this time of the day.

"Good morning, my name is Dr. Pintér," he introduced himself.

"Good morning. I know who you are, please come in." Helen invited him inside.

"Sorry for my appearance, but I am in the middle of cooking lunch," she continued with an apologizing tone in her voice. "I hope you do not mind talking to me in the kitchen."

"It is quite all right," he quickly replied. They went into the large kitchen with a heavy, metal wood-burning stove on the opposite side of the door. Next to the stove, there was a sink with running water. In the middle of the kitchen was a table with five chairs. A large window was facing the courtyard decorated with pretty curtains and a relatively large cupboard neatly arranged with kitchen utensils, dishes, and silverware.

"Please sit down," she offered.

"I have a hard task at hand," Dr. Pintér started off with a big sigh. "As you may know, I am the official guardian of the Jewish boy in Békés living with the Hajdú family and I need to make a recommendation concerning your adoption request," he continued with a calm steady voice.

"I promise you Dr. Pintér, we will not back out from our plan to adopt him," Helen replied with strong conviction. "We will not let a Jewish boy grow up with a Christian family, outside of his faith and outside his destiny. We have the means to raise him in the most proper way."

Before Dr. Pintér could say a word, Helen walked to the door and motioned him to follow her. Dr. Pintér felt some embarrassment since he thought that Helen was asking him to leave the premises.

"Let me show you my house, please." The kitchen was connected to the rest of the house by a long hallway with doors on both sides. The first door on the right was the laundry room, a small room with tiles covering the floor for easy cleanup. An iron stove was standing in the corner next to the window that was facing the backyard. Currently, it was empty with the exception of a large washbasin that was usually used to wash clothes and other hand washable items. The next room was a large room used as a pantry. The walls were covered with shelves all the way to the ceiling. The shelves were packed with bottles, some of them empty and most of them were filled with pickled vegetables and canned fruits. In the middle of the room was a large table covered with sacks filled with various foodstuffs like flower, sugar, etc.

On the left, opposite of the pantry door, a dark solid oak door led into a large room with a podium; this room was completely empty.

"We did not have the chance yet to furnish this room," Helen explained. "We really do not need this room for only the two of us." The adjoining room was separated by a French door and was furnished with several antique wardrobes and a china closet. In the middle of the room, there was a large dining table with six high back chairs. A beautiful fireplace made of tiles was standing in one corner and during the winter, it provided heat for both rooms. The side of the room facing the street had wall-to-wall windows and the opposite side, a glass door and two large windows were facing the terrace bringing in enough light to make both rooms very bright. Another door led to the couple's bedroom. This room also had three large windows facing the street. An antique French bed was standing by the wall facing this door. In addition, two antique wardrobes and a couch with matching armchairs made this room a combination of bedroom and living room. This room was also heated by an eloquent fireplace made of tiles.

So far, Dr. Pintér was astonished. He had rarely seen such a beautiful house. He has not yet seen the rest of the house. He heard some noises coming through the door next to the fireplace.

"Forgive me, Dr. Pintér but our maid is cleaning the bathroom."

"Would you like to see it? I will show you." Of course, he wanted to see it. Another door of this room led into a small hallway with a window and two additional doors. One of the doors led into the toilet with running water (Water Closet or WC), and the other door led to the bathroom completed with a large iron tub with shower head that can be used to take a shower in addition to taking a bath. A wood burning boiler supplied the hot water to the bathtub and to the sink next to it. The young servant girl apologized with a shy smile on her face for the mess she has created. She was in middle of the cleaning the house.

Silently, they headed back to the kitchen. She took a quick look at the stove making sure nothing was burned. Neither of them knew how to break this wall of silence. She was angry about this visit; she was convinced that Dr. Pinter wanted to persuade her and her husband to withdraw their adoption application. Meanwhile, Dr. Pinter was somewhat embarrassed to continue the conversation, because he realized that the adoption of Lacika by the Kádár family was best for this orphaned boy. He was speechless maybe for the first time in his long career, a somewhat unusual phenomenon for a lawyer.

The silence was finally broken by some noises coming from outside. Ede had just come home. Dr. Pintér jumped up from his chair like a kid who had just been surprised in the act doing something forbidden.

"Good Day, Mr. Kádár! I was looking for you in your office and I thought I would talk to your wife until you got back." He found himself talking and unable to stop.

"I do not conduct any business in my house," Ede said to him with a commanding voice, "If you want to talk, let us go to my office." Ede led him into his office through the big empty room that the lawyer just had seen a few minutes ago. Again, he admired the marble columns between the two joining rooms. Ede's office was not big, but still very impressive. Bookshelves full of books were covering one wall. In one corner, there was an antique desk with various carvings on the legs and the front. Ede sat down into the comfortable looking office chair.

"Basically, I wanted to tell you that I will support your adoption application and I will let the authorities know that I have no objections," the lawyer uncomfortably spitted out the words.

"You should understand Mr. Kádár that the Hajdú family loves the child and they spent the last couple of years loving and supporting Lacika," Dr. Pintér continued. "They are just scraping by, should they get some kind of compensation for their effort?"

"Now I understand why you are here," Ede snapped at him. "You want to extort money from me. You want my money to buy your to support of my adoption plan!"

"No, no it is not that," the lawyer protested desperately. "Eszti and János are good people and they deserve some money for their good deed."

"Did the Hajdú family put you up to this?" Ede asked him.

"They have no idea that I am talking to you about this," Dr. Pintér gingerly stated.

"I thought they were taking care of Lacika because of their good heart and love of this child?"

"Yes, but they are poor people. They need money to compensate the hardship caused by the extra mouth to feed."

"All right, I will pay them. You will let me know how much money would be acceptable and I will pay them after we get the boy."

Dr. Pintér said goodbye and left his office in the hurry. He had gotten what he wanted. Now Dr. Pintér can go and tell the Hajdú family to give up on contesting the adoption process and they would be compensated nicely for their effort. Their effort to stop the adoption would probably be futile anyway. Might as well get some money while they walking away from the child.

"Was this strange?" Ede told his wife after he returned from his office. "Do you understand why he came to speak to us?"

"I think initially he wanted to convince us to give up the child," Helen speculated, "but I guess after he saw our house, our social status, our financial situation, he decided not to pursue it."

"Great," Ede said, "our Budapest office just forwarded the petition by the Hajdú family to block my adoption of Lacika. They were asking my advice on what they should do with the petition" he continued. After this, Ede went back to his office and made a call to someone in the Budapest office. After he finished the call, Ede went back to his wife to eat his lunch.

"I just got off the phone with Budapest and they told me that they would not interfere in this matter." Ede never told Helen about the money he promised to pay to the Hajdú family. Why should he make her upset? Let us just enjoy the new addition to the house and hope for a bright future.

§ § § § §

Eszti was mad. She was frustrated, she was angry as hell. From any government office where she tried to block the adoption, she was dismissed. Even the lawyer, her trusted advisor, Dr. Pintér told her to give up the fight.

"Why can't I succeed with this?" she yelled to her husband. "You are in the police department, how come you cannot find anyone who can help us? Why it is so difficult to find anyone we could ask or bribe to help us to win our fight?"

"I guess we are too insignificant to make any difference." János was standing front of his wife quietly, helplessly. He had no idea why his wife felt so attached to this boy. He too loved Lacika, but his feelings towards him were not as strong as Eszti's. By no means did he want to give up the boy, but he knew that if people on the top made up their minds people like him have no chance to win. On the other hand, he could not bear to see his wife suffer and he decided to try to do something. On the pretense of going to work, he went to visit Dr. Pintér.

"Dr. Pintér," János started, "I did not tell my wife that I came to see you, but I was debating what to do about Lacika. We are working people, we do not have much."

"What are you trying to tell me?" the lawyer asked János.

"I was thinking if it would be possible, maybe we could get some kind of payment for our effort raising Lacika." János had a hard time explaining his intentions of making some money out of the situation.

"Why are you asking this, János? Did you forget already that I was helping you with your expenses?"

"Forgive me Dr. Pintér, but we should be paid for our work of raising the child who was not ours!" János started to gain more confidence, since he sensed the lawyer was in agreement with him.

"I will talk to Mr. Kádár," Dr. Pintér suggested. He did not want to tell János the truth that he already knew that some money would be coming. Dr. Pintér, at this time, had no idea how much money would be appropriate compensation.

§ § § § § §

In the meantime, Eszti also decided to do something. Without her husband's knowledge, she was looking to do something, something more daring. She went to the county's Bureau of Orphan's Welfare in Gyula, the county seat. She had only a limited level of education. As many women in her age she finished only six-grade elementary school, the minimum schooling required by the Hungarian Education system. She had no chance of winning but she was a very determined woman.

"May I see Dr. Kardos, the chairman?" Eszti asked the receptionist.

"What is your purpose in talking to him?"

"I must talk to him about my son László Földvári."

The receptionist told her to wait and she went to see if Dr. Kardos would talk to Eszti.

"Please walk right in," she waived to Eszti. She got encouraged by overcoming her first hurdle. She will be able talk to the right person about her situation and could explain what she wants regarding Lacika.

"I sent an application to block the adoption of Lacika by the Kádár family," Eszti told Dr. Kardos.

Since Dr. Kardos did not say anything Eszti continued.

"I never received any acknowledgment from this office or any other office that I sent my application. Please tell me, what is going on? Why is everyone ignoring us?" Eszti impatiently spitted out these worlds.

Dr. Kardos was puzzled about this woman's courage to fight for her cause. He was not used to hear this kind of pushy, forward speaking people. The people that came to see him would be humble and respectful. He paused for minute before he answered.

"Look my good woman, there are forces that are much stronger than you and me. These people are controlling the future of this case," he started calmly. "My dear women, please, go home and forget about your fight. Neither you nor I could stop this adoption. I am very familiar with this unusual case. I am sorry about your loss." Dr. Kardos calmly but firmly spoken so there would not be any misunderstandings.

Tears had started to form in Eszti's eyes. She realized that it was time for her to give up Lacika and hope that he would move toward a good and stable future.

"Thank you Sir for your time," Eszti whispered and slowly walked out from the office. For a while, she wondered aimlessly on the streets of Gyula. She somehow ended up by the railroad station and took the train home.

6

the family

Lacika had been living with the Hajdú family for over a year and was now three years old. By this time, his life was relatively stable with the surrogate family, which until now had been the only family he knew. He and his "siblings" were living together as if they were brothers and sisters. The children did not care nor understand that one of them was an outsider. Lacika, at this juncture of his life, was too young to realize that he was not a natural child of the Hajdú family. He called Eszti Mama, and in return, Eszti gave him love. As far as Lacika knew, he was her son. Lacika was a baby when this family took him in. The relatively peaceful times in this small town helped the family to raise their children in a pleasant and stable family environment.

Food supply and medical care was still not adequately provided for everyone. Lacika was reasonably healthy, but he was skinny and fragile. His main source of food, and his favorite, was bread with smoked bacon and a glass of warm milk. This kind of diet was not necessarily a perfect source of kosher food nor was it a well balanced diet. In those days, people ate whatever food they were able to get. Nobody knew the concept of "a well balanced diet." Fresh vegetables were available only in the summer, thus the sources of necessary vitamins were not readily available year-around. Many young and old people had health issues as a result and malnutrition was common. Like many other children, Lacika too was suffering from malnutrition.

The Hajdú family belonged to the Protestant Church, but they were not much of a church-going people. They went to church for weddings, funerals, christenings and some other special occasions. Lacika did not have a great deal of exposure to any religion, nor did he care about it at the age of three.

§ § § § § §

It was a miserable cold winter morning. Overnight, a big storm dropped over 50 centimeter (20 inches) of show. It was cold, about -10C° (14F°,) and most people stayed home if they could. A heavy layer of snow covered the street, the houses, and the trees. The neighborhood was wrapped in a layer of this white stuff as if the snow cover were part of a large down blanket. The sun carefully peeked out from its own snow-like blanket made of puffy white clouds. Its sparkling rays warmed up the air on the top of the snow and the snow started to melt a little bit, but the air was way too cold and as soon as a small cloud blocked the sun's rays, the top of the snow blanket refroze again. When the sun peeked out again, its rays made the refrozen snow sparkle as if they were made of tiny diamonds. This phenomenon made the outside a little bit more inviting. For an observer this serene scene was a sight to be remembered.

The quiet scene was suddenly disturbed by the engine noise of an approaching automobile. The wheels of the automobile made cracking noises by tearing down the surface of the untouched snow, making a sound as if someone was smashing glasses at a brick wall. The wheels drew long parallel lines in the fresh snow creating an illusion of a train track.

The noise of the car made Lacika curious and he carefully peeked out the window, but not before, he scraped off some of the frost that had built on the window glass with his nails. The thin layer of frost, which looked like snow flowers, was formed by the warm humid air inside meeting the freezing cold window glass. Lacika's effort was well worth it, he observed a big black automobile approaching on the street and stopping at the front of their house. The set of long straight lines created by the tires of the car on the undisturbed white snow amused the child. He was excited to see the black automobile in front of his house. Cars and trucks were hardly ever seen on this small side street. Automobiles were beyond the average person's dreams in those days. Most automobiles were used only by government officials and only a few locals had enough money to afford an automobile. Most side streets of the town were not paved. Why should they be paved? After all motor vehicle traffic was negligible, thus there was no reason to do so. The horse drawn carriages were able to navigate any street in the town. The street where Lacika was living had only paved sidewalks. Occasionally, horse drawn carriage would come around delivering goods like coal or firewood. Seeing an automobile was a special treat for Lacika. He could not even dream to be inside in one of these strange looking fabrications.

A policeman along with a man and a woman got out from the car. The driver stayed inside the vehicle. They knocked on the door and Lacika was excited. Not too many visitors ever came to their house and even when someone did come to visit, none of them ever came with an automobile. Lacika was sure that these people must be very important. After they came into the house, he heard the grownups talking in the hallway, but did not hear what was being said. He was curious, but was afraid to come out from the other room. His brothers and sisters were also excited seeing strangers and they were whispering to each other wondering what these people were doing in their house. Soon the mystery was solved. Mama came into the children's room and hugged Lacika unusually hard. Lacika noticed tears in her eyes.

"Mama, why are you crying?" he asked, fighting off his own tears. "What's happening? Who are these strange people?" Mama was hugging him and did not say a word. Now Lacika started to weep, but he had no idea why was he crying.

"Lacika…please do not cry," Mama was wiping her own eyes, "be a good boy and we'll see you soon." Now all the children gathered around Lacika as if they wanted to protect him from the strangers.

The woman gently took away Lacika from Mama's arm and away from his siblings. The grownups were still talking to each other. Lacika could not understand what they were talking about because he was so scared. He had no idea what was happening. He felt miserable. He sensed something different about today. He knew today was the day when his life was changing. He did not want any changes. He did not want to be a part of whatever it was happening. This was the only life he ever knew and he liked it here. He heard when those strange people saying goodbye to Mama. The woman and the man started to leave the house and his mother was staying! The woman put a warm coat on Lacika. He was held by the woman's arm while they all left the house. They got into the big automobile with the exception of the policeman, who walked away on foot. The woman was still holding onto Lacika. Lacika would have enjoyed the ride under different circumstances, but now he was scared.

"Why is Mama not coming with me?" He wandered and got even more frightened. The woman was smiling at him, but this gesture did not calm him down.

"I have to get out of here," Lacika told himself, then with all his strength he pushed hard into the chest of the woman and tried to free himself to run home to Mama.

"Let me go!" he screamed, "I want Mama, I want my mother. I WANT MAMA!" he yelled hysterically. He started to kick and scream more and more violently until the woman was unable to hold on to him anymore. The man finally grabbed him with authority and he too tried to hold down the panic-stricken child. The man with a soft, but firm voice tried to reason with him, but Lacika was so much too enraged and did not hear a single word the man was trying to say to him. The car doors were closed and the automobile started to move, slowly leaving the house behind. Lacika looked out the back window and saw Mama by the sidewalk, wiping her eyes from her tears and waiving to him. Lacika kept his eyes on his Mama until the car slowly turned into the main street and sped away.

From all the excitement and fighting Lacika became very tired; the gentle motions of the car made him drowsy and slowly he fell asleep. The heavy snow covered roads made their 10-kilometer trip last a long time. It was after noon by the time they arrived at the Kádár family residence. The man gently carried the small boy to the house and laid him down on their bed. He took off his coat and shoes while Lacika was sleeping deep and dreaming of home and Mama. Ede went to work and left Lacika in Helen's care.

§ § § § § §

Lacika started to wake up, but he continued to pretend to sleep and did not want to open his eyes to face reality. He was not sure what just happened to him. Was it real or only a dream? He was hoping it was a bad dream that would go away when he opened his eyes. He remembered some strange people dressed in dark clothes, a big black automobile, going away somewhere, saying goodbye Mama. Was it real or only a dream? He was hoping it was a bad dream that would go away when he opened his eyes. At this moment, he was not sure, nor did he want to know. All his life, this never explained dream, or dreamlike event would haunt him. Since nobody ever talked to him about this event, he would never be sure if it was a bad dream or a real event. He found out the truth only much later in his life.

Now, Lacika was uncertain about today's events, but he was very comfortable. After awhile, he felt that someone was looking at him, but he was afraid to open his eyes. He decided to stay quiet for a little bit more.

She was watching the little boy while he was sleeping. He had a cute round face, high forehead suggesting that this child may be a smart boy. His face also showed a great deal of suffering. These times were trying times for everyone especially for children. Children were innocent bystanders of these unkind times. Young children, even older people could not explain why the world was so cruel for its citizens.

This boy was an innocent by-product of a violent era trapped between evil and good. Her untrained eye noticed how undernourished Lacika was, very skinny and fragile looking. This child badly needs love, to be taken care of, to be happy. Her heart as a mother opened up for the little boy. At this moment, she knew that her long awaited son had arrived. There will be so many things to do. Lacika hardly had any appropriate clothes and shoes, toys and other things that a child might need. She had to get all this as soon as possible. She was not ready for this responsibility. The decision to take him home was made too fast for Helen. One may ask when would be a new mother be ready for a child? We all know the truth: none of them ever was. She was anxious; she wanted to brag about her newly found child. These thoughts gave her a rush, excitement, hope for a happy future. She would no longer be left alone all day, while her husband was away working. It seems now she has more reason, more purpose to be hopeful for a happy life in the future. A new chapter in her life has started.

Finally, Lacika opened his eyes. He looked at Helen with an intense curiosity. It seemed that this strange woman was still a part of his bad dream. He wanted to make sure he was awake. He gently touched her face and asked:

"Are you real? Am I still asleep? Where am I? Who are you? Why I am here?" Lacika did not realize that all these questions came out from his mouth at once. He thought that his dream was continuing and he was saying these words in his sleep. He did not expect any answers from Helen. Helen too, was not sure what was happening in Lacika's mind. Lacika felt calm, had a strange relaxed feeling, of course he does. He was in the middle of a dream. Was he? If he was not, why did he no longer feel the shaky, nervous, rejecting feelings anymore? Maybe he was too tired to resist. Lacika did not realize that this place would be his home from this point on. Then, suddenly Lacika realized he was awake, all of his senses were operational, and he was definitely missing his Mama. He could not remember a time when he was away from Mama.

"Where is Mama?" he asked Helen with a sad face. He was expecting an answer.

"She will visit you soon, Lacika," Helen replied. "Lacika," she wondered to herself. It was so strange to say his name. "Is this really the name of my son?" Helen with an impulse hugged the child.

"This was so nice," Lacika thought. "She smells so good. Her hands are so soft!" Mama's hands were always rough from her work around the house.

They were in the bedroom and Lacika was lying on a large French bed. The bed felt very soft, comfortable, and spacious. He has never experienced the soft touch of a bed like this and it felt very inviting. No wonder if he did not feel like getting up. The tall tile stove was lit in the corner and made this large beautiful bedroom comfortably warm and cozy. The cracking sound of the fire, the flickering light from the flames reflecting on the darkening room ceiling made the whole scene very serene and it had a calming effect on Lacika. Lacika again felt very relaxed. He still did not understand what was happening to him, but somehow it felt so comfortable to be here now.

The short winter day was almost over. The sun had already passed the horizon and it would be dark soon. The sun disappeared leaving behind a red half-circle painted on the horizon.

He felt hungry, but he was afraid to ask for anything. Indeed, he felt so comfortable that he did not want to move at all.

Helen was watching the child and she was so absorbed watching him that she completely forgot the time, and did not realize that this child did not have anything to eat for most of the day.

"Lacika, are you hungry? Would you like to eat something?" Helen carefully asked him. "Is there anything that you would like to eat?" She asked Lacika again, without getting any reaction from him.

Lacika was not accustomed to this kind of questioning. Mama always knew what to give him to eat. Helen was wondering what a three-year-old child would usually eat. The reality hit her again. She was not ready to take care of a child. She was familiar with the fact that there was no schooling available to learn how to raise a child, but under normal circumstances, this was a process. Normally, parents would go through this learning process slowly. The new parents learn as they go and constantly make corrections on mistakes they make. In this situation, this process was skipped entirely and she was jumping right into the middle of being a parent. It was not too long ago that she was taking care of her own brothers and sisters after her father died. True, her mother was there to help, but she still should remember those times. Today, Helen has a maid who helps in her housework. Today, her life was so much better than in her childhood. She still could do it.

The realization of her chosen responsibility, gave her a burst of energy. She always has been very handy in the kitchen. Even though the maid was helping, Helen still did most of the cooking. She was not sure if she should leave Lacika in the bedroom alone or take him with her. Lacika looked so comfortable, so she told him that she would be right back with some food.

Lacika was left alone. He was not frightened anymore. Somehow, he felt comfortable in this big wonderful room. He had never been in or seen such a nice room before. He got up from the bed and went to look out the window. The snow was still covering the ground. The reflections of the streetlights on the white snow seemed to change the color of the snow to pink. There was a big empty square across the street. He was wondering about this park. This park seemed a perfect place to use his wooden sled if his brothers would be with him. Then he turned his attention to the room. He went to the tile stove touched it gently it felt nice and warm. He hugged it and he felt so warm all over. This was new to him, too. He has seen one before, but he did not know what it was. There was a large table in the middle of the room. He went over and sat down on one of the high backed chairs. He felt with his hands the nice cushiony seat of the chair; it was so comfortable to sit on it. In Mama's house the chairs were made of all wood, he never realized that sitting on a chair could be so nice and comfy. Helen walked in with a tray in her hand full of goodies. The food smelled good, he was extremely hungry.

"Well Lacika you have to wash your hands before you eat," Helen said to him, grabbed his hand, and led him to the bathroom. Lacika could not believe his eyes, there was a container or something hanging on the wall. She has done something and like magic, warm water was pouring into this container. Mama usually warmed up some water on the stove, and then poured the water into a pail for the kids to wash their hands and faces. Here, the water was coming from the wall inside the house.

"Where does the water coming from?" Lacika got up his nerve to ask.

"It comes from a well outside of the house," she replied.

"How does the water come into the house?" he asked again and looked behind the container.

"There are pipes that are connected to the well." He kept asking question after question. Helen had a hard time keeping up with answers. Lacika never stopped asking questions for most of his life.

After washing his hands and face, they went back to the other room. For the first time today, he finally recognized something that was familiar to him: food. He drunk some warm milk and ate fresh buttered bread with some jam on it. Then he had some delicious cookies which before he had only on special occasions. He was almost finished eating when the man came home. Lacika did not pay much attention to him before and he was not too happy about the way the man had restrained him in the car while they were coming to this house. He was a tall man with a kind smile on his face. His black hair was combed straight back, exposing a high forehead. He kissed the woman as he walked into the room. Lacika assumed that they must be husband and wife.

The two adults started to talk and for a while, they were completely ignoring Lacika. Lacika did not mind it. He was totally consumed with eating his cookies and paid absolutely no attention to the couple. When Lacika finished eating, Helen asked him if he would like to go to sleep, it was getting late. Lacika found it interesting that she asked him instead of being told to go to sleep. He did not resist going to sleep. He was tired, exhausted from the day's events. Helen helped him into his nightshirt and she made up the couch by the window for him to sleep on. Lacika felt a little bit uneasy sleeping in a bed by himself. This was the first time ever he did not have to share a bed. The couch was soft and inviting and in no time, he was fast asleep.

The couple was discussing today's events. They both felt good about their decision of getting this small child. The long battle to make the adoption legal was just starting. Lacika was here and now Helen and Ede can plan for a future that included this child. They both agreed that they would never tell Lacika about his adoption. They figured after some time, this young child would completely forget his past and there would be no reason to remind him of the truth. Why open up wounds unnecessarily? They were hoping that the Hajdú family would disappear from their lives and nothing will remind Lacika of the past.

§ § § § §

It is hard to argue against the decision not to tell Lacika about his adoption and the fact that he was not their biological child. Everyone should know that both Ede and Helen raised him as their "real" child,

Lacika never suspected anything. Why should he know the truth? What could Lacika gain with this knowledge? His birth parents had never been found, nobody ever came to claim him. Ede and Helen gave him their undivided love and provided him with the best in everything that they were able to give. He loved them in return. Lacika always was a good child and respected them just as much as any other child in those days would.

On the other hand, should not a child know where he has come from?

7

early days

More than a year has passed since Lacika moved into the spacious house of Helen and Ede. During this time, it seemed the adoption process would never be completed. Once in awhile, Ede tried to inquire about the reason for the delay but nobody would gave him a straight answer. The most likely reason for the delay was that the courts were busy with other "more important" cases; in their opinion, a minor matter like an adoption could wait. Ede was truly not concerned about this delay. Lacika was living with them and everything else was unimportant. Finally, in January 1948, Ede received a notice to appear before the adoption hearing at the county court in Gyula on February 17, 1948. The hearing was short and it was merely a formality as the last phase of the adoption process. By the time of the hearing, the courts had already approved the adoption. In front of two witnesses, Dr. Pintér, as the official guardian of László Földvári, signed over the adoption certificate to Ede and Helen Kádár. Lacika finally officially joined the Kádár family. Everyone was happy and some friends came by to congratulate the Kádár family and wish them the best of luck. After the adoption, Ede hired a professional photographer and took many pictures to keep this event not only as a good memory, but to create visual memorabilia of the joyful event.

The life of Lacika with Ede and Helen slowly became routine; a life like any other four-year-old child would normally have. It was not so difficult to get used to a good life. Eszti came by a few times; Lacika was happy to see her, he was crying after she left. As time went by, Lacika felt a sense of belonging in his new home. For a while, Lacika was happy to see Mama, but later on, he could hardly wait to get back to his toys and newly found friends. The new life became his life; he started to forget all about Mama and his siblings.

Maybe, Lacika wanted to forget his previous life, a life he left far behind somewhere with not too many good memories. Maybe a child's memories were lost because those memories no longer meant anything anymore to Lacika. His life was wonderful now; he did not want to change it for the world. Why should he? This place was his home and these people were his family, these parents were his parents, who love him dearly.

§ § § § § §

By the year 1948, the country was in turmoil again. The wind from the "EAST" was sweeping the country. The Soviet Union's influence on the Hungarian political and economic life became more and more apparent. The country was still in the process of rebuilding after the devastating effects of the war. Interestingly, Hungary as whole was on the road to recovery much better than most of the other European countries that were on the losing side of the war. However, shortages of all kinds of goods were constant due to political and organizational disarray. The Hungarian government badly needed funds to rebuild the country, but money was in short supply for everyone, for both the general population and for the central and local government agencies. Western countries still had their own economic problems. The Americans helped to rebuild most Western European countries including West Germany; they helped to better the lives of people after the devastating war. The US used this political move for their advantage. The USA wanted to strengthen their ties with the Western allies and to unite these countries against the Soviet Union's expansionist politics. For obvious reasons, the Americans would not help any country that was under the iron grip of the Soviet Union. The government of the Soviet Union also badly needed financial help to rebuild their own country, where the human and material devastation was much higher than in any other countries involved in the war. Even more than three years after the war, the people of the Soviet Union were still suffering due to the devastating losses endured during the war. The Soviet Union had special plans for the countries they "liberated." These newly occupied countries were lined up to fulfill a greater goal of world domination. The war helped Stalin, the dictator of the Soviet Union, to carry out the goal of increasing control over bordering countries like Poland, Romania, Czechoslovakia, Hungary, and the eastern part of Germany. In addition, they also took hold of the Baltic countries like Estonia, Lithuania, and Latvia. They tried unsuccessfully to take control of Finland, too. The Soviet Union purposely created political instability in these satellite countries to make life unnecessarily difficult for the general population and delay their economic progress. People were told that the reason for their current suffering was the capitalist west. The western capitalists did not want the poor, hardworking proletariat and their co-sufferers, the peasants, to succeed because they were afraid of the "workers" power, which would eliminate the capitalists' domination and exploitation of the working class. The reality was that the Soviet Union took all measures to assure improving their own economy using goods from the so-called "Warsaw Pack" countries. Most common food items were rationed. Certain items, sometimes even basic groceries, could only be obtained with a ration-booklet issued to every family. These ration books only allowed families to obtain predetermined, minimal quantities of foodstuff. On the other hand, people with money could buy everything on the black-market for a high price.

The Soviet Union political machinery was working in the background using local Communist party members in most Hungarian cities and towns. These new Communists were trained, sometimes (many times,) brainwashed during their imprisonment in prison/labor camps in Siberia. The leadership worked hard to recruit as many communist sympathizers as possible. The final goal was to recruit enough people to create a majority, a majority that would support without any hesitation the establishment of a Soviet style communism and create a force that would help the Soviet Union to set up foundation for controlling Hungary's political and economic system. The communists were not choosy. The Nazis party was abolished after the war, but the old members of "Arrow Cross" (Nyilas) party joined the local police forces, the secret police (AVH), and many other communist agencies. Indeed, the communists preferred most of these scum, since they were well trained in the brutal interrogation of innocent people, just as the Communist dictatorship's own people were. Let us be honest, these people did not care who they beat up, their brutality was made their life a pleasure. The good Nazis had become even better communists.

§ § § § § §

János, Eszti's husband, came from a working class family, a true proletariat. This kind of background was looked upon favorably by the Communists. As an experienced policeman, he was successfully recruited by the communists. János spent a great deal of time with his newly found comrades, friends, and drinking buddies. Now his job was to beat-up and torture people. Frequently, he got drunk to forget his deeds, and got drunk to enable him to do these horrible deeds again on the next day.

Eszti had to take care of her family without any help from her husband. She too realized that under these circumstances, she had to give up Lacika for good and slowly stopped her visits. She also realized that Lacika, a small innocent child who had no control over his own life, had found a comfortable home with loving parents and was happy there. With a heavy heart, with a great deal of hesitation, she wrote her last letter to Helen to say goodbye to Lacika.

Dear Mrs. Kádár!

Thank you for the latest gift package sent by the Adoptions Agency, we are really appreciating it.

It gives me pain knowing that Lacika suffered so much after I left him with you. Believe me, I cannot sleep at night, I cannot do my work during the day. The lovely face of Lacika is always in front of me and I feel that part of my heart was lost. I do not want to stir up any more suffering for him. I ask G-d to give peace to Lacika's heart and to me.

I am asking you please take care of Lacika so he will never suffer again. If his real mother would ever be found, please do not give him away, if you do not want to keep him anymore, give him back to me. Please make sure that he never will forget me. Let him know that I will love him forever.

For you, my dear Lacika I pray for G-d to surround you with people who will love you as much as I did. Goodbye, with love and kisses

Your little Mother

PS. Please send me the photos of Lacika when they are ready. Please send me updates about Lacika whenever it is possible.

Best regards

Eszti Hajdú

Sept 31. 1947

§ § § § §

Lacika never had any friends before he came to his new home. Why would he ever want to have any other friends when he had brothers and sisters? Numerous people were visiting the Kádár family, many came because of curiosity and to see their new son and wish them good luck. Of course, close friends of Ede and Helen come by also, but these friends would visit them because they were friends of the family. Lacika liked when these friend came by, because he was the center of attention during their visits.

Lacika carefully observed these new people. They were so different from the ones he had met in the past. For example, there was a man with a funny looking long white beard with long curly sideburns. His name was Uncle Yayli. He always wore a dark hat and even when he took off his hat, he wore a funny looking little cap on his head, which he would never take off. He did not have much hair and Lacika figured this little cap was to keep his head warm, because it would cover his boldness. Uncle Yayli's wife was a short stocky woman with a lot of energy. The ancient Latin language expression: perpetuum-mobile (perpetual motion) could well describe her behavior. Most of her energy concentrated around her mouth, her mouth acted like a machine that would never stop. For Lacika, she seemed to be much younger than her husband was and maybe that was the reason she seemed to be so energetic next to the old Uncle Yayli. Lacika always remembered Uncle Yayli as a perpetual old man. Was he? The long white beard did not help to dismiss the mystery of his oldness. Truly, he was not much older than Ede. He too was a survivor of a concentration camp, Buchenwald. He was the sole survivor of his family; he lost his wife and seven children; maybe his loss of happiness was the reason why he looked so old. His current wife was also a Holocaust survivor. They got married after the war. Indeed, she was much younger. These kinds of marriages were not unique in the Jewish communities; everybody wanted to belong to someone. Both of them were beyond childbearing age. She had never been married before and she too longed for a child of her own. Lacika was the closest reality to her dreams. Now Uncle Yayli seemed to be content. He had his synagogue, a community that respected and loved him he had his wife… Well two out three was a good thing.

These two people visited the Kádár family frequently and they seemed to develop affection towards Lacika. They had the patience to play with him. They often brought toys for him as if they wanted to buy his love.

In his young age, Lacika noticed an interesting interaction between the husband and wife. She was snappy and short. Obviously, she was wearing the "pants" in the house. Uncle Yayli usually sat quietly with a shy smile on his face and listened to the conversations. Was he listening? Nobody could ever be sure, if his mind was wandering around or if he was really listening. He was a man of few words. For a casual bystander, he seemed to be a man without a nerve. He had a few compulsive habits that Lacika noticed with some interest. One of the funniest things was the way Uncle Yayli was stroking his beard. He grabbed his chin between this thumb and index finger, and then slowly moved his hand down on his beard until his hand reached the end of his long white beard. He repeated this activity slowly many-many more times. After awhile, Lacika was guessing, he got bored with this activity and stopped stroking his beard. He needed to do something else with his hand. His next activity was to curl his long sideburns by tightly rolling it around his index finger and quickly releasing it. He would do this numerous times on both sides, before giving it up and going back to stroking his beard. His bashful smile would never leave his face, no matter what he was doing. Lacika was fascinated by this since he was the first man with a long beard that he had ever seen up close.

There were others, mostly Jewish families, visiting the Kádár family. These people had babies and small children. Most of these kids were younger than Lacika with a few exemptions. It was commonly known that very few Jewish children survived Hitler's final solution. Lacika was born during the war so he was one the oldest children in the Jewish community of Békéscsaba. Only a few Jewish families had children close to Lacika's age and they wanted their child to have Jewish playmates. The Friedman family had a cute little girl named Kati a year younger than Lacika. The two kids instantly became friends starting at the first moment they met, they were running around, and playing together as old friends would. Unfortunately, the Friedman family lived on the other side of the city and the kids did not have that many chances to play together. Lacika also enjoyed visiting the Friedman family at their house. The yard of the house looked like a big park with fruit trees and a vegetable garden. When in season, the kids were picking strawberries, raspberries, apples, and cherries right from the trees, bushes, and wherever else they would find anything edible. This friendship would last for many years to come. After 1956, the Friedman family, along with many others, immigrated to Israel and the Kádár family lost contact with them.

Another friend of Ede was the Bánki family. They had son, Géza, who was about two years old and a one-year-old baby girl named Ági. The two families often visited each other; there was a strong bond between the adults. Lacika was not too crazy about Géza, but when they were together, they both behaved as civilized human beings; as much as a two and four year old would, their friendship also lasted for many years.

§ § § § § §

In early spring of 1948, Lacika started to call Helen MAMA. She was so happy with this; finally, her son had become her SON. Eszti's visitations became less and less frequent and finally stopped alto-gether. Helen openly told Ede that she did not like these visits. Ede agreed, but he did not want to do anything to stop these visits. Helen felt uncomfortable when Eszti was around Lacika and unconsciously Helen truly despised these visits. She made it harder and harder to agree to these short meetings, Helen found reasons to postpone and delay the visits of Eszti. Intuitively, Helen felt that Lacika would be better off forgetting Eszti. Lacika did not need a constant remainder of his previous life. It worked. It worked, because Eszti had to drag herself all the way from Békés with the train to Békéscsaba and if the Kádár family was not home, she had to go back and try again on another time, wasting at least half a day in the process. Her life in general was not so easy. She could not afford the loss of a half-day pay just to see a child who was drifting away from her.

The new life of Lacika became the ordinary life for Lacika, he felt right at home. The life here was so much different from his life with the Hajdú family. After about a year, Lacika stopped thinking about his previous life and slowly forgot it all. After Eszti stopped her visits, there was nothing to remind him about his past. This "memory loss" was directly related to the fact that Eszti stayed away from Lacika. According to Helen, this greatly benefited Lacika; it was the best thing for him.

With the Kadar family, Lacika was exposed to many strange new customs that he had never seen before. These daily routines slowly developed into an integral part of his life. In the beginning, for a young boy of three, these customs were burdensome and meaning-less. Later in his life, these restrictions and responsibilities were even more of a nuisance; it separating him from the rest of the kids his age and made him a target of discrimination. On the other hand, Lacika understood that this was the price to be a Jew. Later in life, he learned that religion represents only a small component of being Jewish. Lacika discovered the Jewish contributions to science, art, literature, and medicine; he was proud to be a Jew and religion was treated as an old tradition that needed to be preserved and respected.

The daily life of young Lacika was filled with many responsibilities. Before the Kádár family started to eat, Ede washed his hand and made everyone do the same. Washing ones hand before eating was not so strange, but what followed the hand washing was. After washing his hand, Ede would say some kind of prayer in a language Lacika never heard before. After all the prayers were completed, the family finally started to eat. Ede made sure that his head and Lacika's head was covered at all times. Ede had cap with hard flap on the front and he was always wearing this cap at home. In public, Ede was wearing a regular hat. Wearing a hat was not considered so unusual in those days since most men wore hats outside of their house, but wearing something on someone's head indoors, Lacika found this funny. With a multi-colored scarf, his new Mama also covered her head at all times. This custom of covering everyone's head was completely different than from where Lacika came from. Especially men would not sit down to eat with their head covered. Indeed this act would be considered impolite, disrespectable.

The Kádár family also went to a funny looking "church" mostly on Friday nights and on Saturday mornings. The first time they went, Lacika was a little bit frightened seeing all the strange people who were greeting Ede. The way people looked at Lacika made him incredibly uncomfortable. He met many people, some of whom had long beards just as Uncle Yayli had; he was happy to see a friendly face; some of them were dressed like Ede with their "Sunday" suits. Some of the people were wearing strange looking long jackets Lacika had never seen before. This kind of attire gave the impression to Lacika that they were too "old fashioned." He also noticed that people wearing these clothes had long beards, too. By the way, Uncle Yayli was wearing this kind of clothing in the synagogue. Most of the children attending the synagogue were younger. Lacika also saw numerous kids with long curly sideburns locked into tight curls. Of course, most children dressed just like Lacika.

He felt uncomfortable and hanged onto Ede's hand tightly like a scared little mouse. They sat into a row of seats somewhere near the front of the synagogue and the service started. An older man put a white striped piece of cloth on his head, opened a book, and started to pray and everyone followed his lead.

"What are they doing?" he asked Ede.

"What is happening?" Lacika asked Ede again.

"Lacika, you must be quiet you should not speak during the service," whispered Ede. He should have known better. Lacika and his questions were unstoppable.

"Why is the man in the front yelling?"

"If I cannot speak, why can he yell like this? What is he saying? I do not understand a word he is saying." Lacika kept talking to Ede, but Ede was quiet for the exception that his mouth was moving without any understandable words coming out of it. Lacika found this funny and it made him giggle.

Finally, Lacika lost his patience and started to scream:

"Why can't you answer me?!" Ede was shocked, he had never seen Lacika so angry, and he had always been calm and quiet. What happened?

"Lacika," he answered finally, "you must be quiet at certain times during the services. I will answer all your questions when we get home."

The synagogue was about a ten-minute walk from their house. During the walk, Ede started to explain to Lacika some of the basics of the Jewish religion. Ede came from an orthodox home, but he had never been well versed in Jewish theology. However, as an observing Jew, he knew most of the basic laws and regulations that controlled the religious Jewish life. When he was young, he attended a Jewish school for his religious studies on most afternoons after he came back from the regular public school. Now he must find a way to explain Judaism to this little child.

"Lacika, I know that you have no idea what this religion is." While Ede was talking, he came to a realization that he has no idea how to explain all this to a little child. "Listen Lacika, I promise that every time we go to shul (synagogue in Yiddish), I will try to explain everything I could."

"What is a shul?" Lacika quickly asked.

"That place we just went before," he answered.

"Why do we need to go there?

"Well, a good Jew goes to shul three times a day to pray."

"Why do we need to pray?" Lacika kept asking. "What does "pray" means?"

It was a good thing that by this time they were home. Ede had a little bit of break, so he did not have to answer any more questions today. Helen kissed them on their cheeks as they entered the house and greeted them with "Gut Shabuoth." The lighted candles in all five arms of a large candlestick were flickering on the dining table. The delicious smell of food was in the air. In the anticipation of a good meal, Lacika forgot all his questions. Impatiently, he was waiting for his supper.

The Kádár family's Friday night supper would not start before more prayers were said by Ede and in later years said by Lacika. The "agony" of waiting for the Friday night super was affectionately remembered by Lacika the rest of his life. It was not among the worst memories he ever had, but it was memorable. After all the prayers that needed to be said were completed, the dinner was served. The traditional chicken soup with homemade noodles (occasionally rice) followed by cooked chicken from the soup with some potatoes garnished with peas and carrots was served. With the exception of the garnish, the same chicken soup with chicken (occasionally beef) was served on each and every Friday night. On rare occasions when Lacika went to other people's houses to eat on a Friday night if the host served different food than what Lacika became accustomed to, he always wondered, "What kinds of Jews were these people?"

8
political troubles

June of 1948 brought great changes in Hungarian politics. The Communists manipulated election results and Mátyás Rákosi was elected as the Secretary General of the Hungarian Workers Party (MDP—Magyar Demokrata Párt,) and he took the Prime Minister position, too. The communist terror started or rather continued "legally." The newly "elected" Communist government achieved complete control of the government by eliminating all oppositions, one-way or another. All independent political parties were abolished; their "lucky" members were put in jails, with no specific charges against them. The new government had the luxury of time to fabricate charges against them later. The unlucky ones faced criminal trials with accusations of being traitors to the Hungarian people. Later, the so called "window trials" would bring to "justice" many innocents, among them were their own comrades. These people many of them devout Communist, were found guilty of treason and betrayal. Many of these innocent people were sentenced to long jail terms or were executed because of these trumped up charges. These trials were highly publicized to show the general population that the new government was serious about their ideology and people should realize they must either go along with the new regime or face consequences if they resist.

Jews had been deprived of their rights for centuries. In the late 19th and early 20th centuries, Jews saw an opportunity to change the world. Karl Marx and Friedrich Engels developed "The Communist Manifesto" that became the "bible" of communist ideology. Most Jews historically were leftists and even today, they are still left leaning even in our times. Russian Jews were active participants of the Russian October Revolution in 1917. Eventually, they helped the

Communists take over the Russian government after deposing the Tsars.

In the spring of 1919, following the end of the First World War, many Jews took active part of a brief takeover of the Hungarian government creating a Communist controlled dictatorship that lasted for 100 days. This was the first Communist controlled government in world history.

After WWII, many Jews joined the ranks of Communist with a different rationale than in the past. The Jews knew that anti-Semites and ex-Nazis were hiding within the Communists Party and many more were in hiding all around the countryside. Jews were looking for revenge. Jews were well aware that the Russian style of Communism did not particularly like Jews. Jews were tolerated as long as they accepted and cooperated with the Communist regime. Even the Hungarian Communist Party leader, Mátyás Rákosi, had Jewish origins but this fact was carefully guarded from the public. Getting rid of the hidden Nazis who had already joined the communist regime was a dangerous undertaking. The success was directly dependant on how well the individual ex-Nazi was connected with other high-ranking officials in his chain-of-command. The members of the secret police were given virtually unlimited powers by the new Communist leadership as long as they were following their superior's commands. The members of the secret police were able to use, and were encouraged to use, any means deemed necessary to advance the government's effort to achieve absolute power and to create a completely totalitarian state. After the Communist takeover, the official name of Hungary was changed to the "Hungarian Peoples Republic." The irony of this title was that it gave everyone the false feeling that the everyday people were in power, but in reality, only small groups of zealots were controlling the country. The people on the top would not tolerate any diversions from their Communist Political Ideology, their Economic Policies or any other aspects of life under their rule. People were too frightened to say or do anything what the Communists might interpret as a "counter revolutionary activity." The general population was afraid to talk about politics with their neighbors, with their closest friends or even in front of their own children.

These political changes affected almost everyone. Ede's life was changed too. As soon as the communists took over all the government offices, they made drastic changes in government personnel. They closed all the offices of the Displaced Properties organization and including the local office in Békéscsaba. Ede lost his job, his source of income.

The local communists tried to recruit Ede to join their ranks. They offered several local government job opportunities, but Ede turned down all offers. I have to say, Ede was not your typical Jew, he had never been a run-of-the-mill Jew. He did not want to do anything with the Communist; he detested them and their ideology. As a result, he found himself without a job. Since Ede was an observant Jew, it was close to impossible to find a job where he did not have to work on Saturdays. The five-day workweeks were not yet invented in the 1940s. Unfortunately, turning down the communists caused a serious problem for Ede. In quick succession, a number of events changed the lives of the Kádár family.

In early September of 1948, Ede received a notification from the city government of Békéscsaba that his house was excessively large for one family and instructed him to vacate immediately all the rooms with the exception of one bedroom. Workers showed up a few days later, removed the two doors leading into the large room with the marble columns, and filled the doorframes with red bricks to complete the permanent separation. They let the Kádár family keep one large room, the kitchen, bathroom, toilet, and two small rooms originally used for pantry and laundry. Lacika was frightened having these workers invading the house. By now, he had gotten used to the large rooms and the freedom to roam around. He felt confined, and for some time, he was afraid to walk in the newly created hallway connecting all the rooms from the kitchen to the large room facing the street.

Shortly after, a family moved into the small one room apartment, unoccupied until now. Before the war, this apartment was originally used by the servants. The rest of the house remained empty until a Clinique for pregnant women was opened in Ede's old offices and the big entertainment room.

Ede was out of work. Both Helen and Ede were worried about what the future would bring. This worry would soon be solved, but unfortunately, not the way Ede hoped and imagined.

At approximately 4:30 on a wintry February morning, the family was rudely awakened by the secret police knocking on their door armed with a search warrant. The year was 1949. The government provided many opportunities for these "Agents" to do their job with enormous efficiency. Within a minute, every room in the apartment had been searched. They opened up everything that could be opened and some that could not. They broke the locks and busted in doors without any consideration or hesitation. Wardrobes and kitchen drawers were emptied and their contents thrown all over the floor. Furniture was moved and violently turned over, throwing their contents all over the house. In a matter of minutes, the apartment was unrecognizable. It looked like it was hit by a tornado. Finally, in the long hallway, behind a coat rack that was recently placed in the front of the sealed doorway, one of the men found a handgun. As soon as they "found" the gun, one of the goons grabbed Ede, placed handcuffs on his hands and the group rushed him away.

At the police station, Ede was charged with illegal gun possession. For days, for weeks, for months, Helen had no inkling where her husband had been taken. When Ede was employed by the Displaced Properties office, he had a gun permit, but after he lost his job, he surrendered his gun to the authorities, along with his gun permit. He no longer owned a gun nor did he want to own one.

To plant evidence was a common practice of the Hungarian Secret Police. When everything else failed to indict someone, small token evidence would go far in creating an illusion of legality to arrest and persecute a person for crimes he did not commit.

It took many weeks until finally Helen received a note that Ede had been charged with illegal weapons possession. He was also charged with a very popular and frequently used offence of the era: "enemy of the state." Still Helen had no idea where Ede had been taken. She was not allowed to visit him. They refused any attempt to find out his whereabouts, his condition or when, if ever, he would be released. Helen did not know for sure if Ede is alive. Poor Ede was in a great deal of trouble. So was Helen.

§ § § § §

With tears in her eyes, Helen looked around the house. Not one piece of furniture was standing where they should be standing, some of them were broken, and all of them were emptied of their contents. What would be next? The winter was almost over, but old man winter still kept his strong grip on the cold. It was a cold on this horrible day. Helen suddenly realized that it was very cold in the house. Lacika was still wearing his pajamas and he was shivering from cold, hunger, and fright from the experience of seeing his father arrested and taken away.

"He must be hungry," crossed her mind, actually she started to feel some hunger pains. It was still before noon, but it seemed to her that an awful long time had passed since they took her husband away.

"I should cook something for lunch," Helen mumbled to herself, "but it would take too much time cook." Then she went to the kitchen and started the fire in the stove. At least the kitchen will be warm. Luckily, she had some bread left over from the day before. She buttered a few slices, found some cheese, and hard-boiled eggs. The sandwiches were ready. Some warmed up milk would complete their breakfast meal. She was kind of surprised herself, how calm she was. She kept telling herself over, and over again: "I will be strong!"

"I will make it!"

"I have to be strong!"

"I have to make it!" Yes, she had to make it without her husband. Who knows if she will ever see her husband again! She was now responsible for herself and her child. She tried to convince herself that solving today's problem would be easier than surviving the concentration camp. G-d will help.

"At this stage of my life, I do not have a job. My health is fragile from the after effects of spending many months in the concentrations camps. I have to frequent doctors for treatments of various health issues. But, my small child needs my loving care." All these thought gave her the strength to be defiant and strong. "Could I restart my life again? How could I do that? Would I ever see my husband again?" These were good questions, but there were no immediate answers.

Lacika was confused, lost. Abruptly, he found himself alone without anyone else but his mother. Helen was constantly crying. It was difficult for Helen to explain to the small child what had happened. She could not even explain to herself. She was confused and felt helpless. She had no idea what she should or could do. She heard many rumors about people in similar situations, where family members were taken away and never heard from again. She also anticipated that her friends would be too frightened to step forward and help her. They too could be in trouble for helping anyone who was labeled as an "enemy of the state." All looked so hopeless.

§ § § § §

The news of Ede's arrest quickly spread throughout the small Jewish community. Fellow Jews were concerned about Helen, but they were also afraid for themselves. The government made sure that these opposition "crack downs" were well advertized among the general population. After Tito, the Communist leader of Yugoslavia, broke away from the control of the Soviet Bloc, Moscow made sure that none of the satellite countries in their grip would follow Tito's example. The government's "public relations" organization stepped up the pace of distributing their rhetoric. They were constantly, relentlessly broadcasting their intent of stopping everyone who was even thinking of "betraying" the authority of the mighty Soviet Union and dare to sway away in their political believes from the mainstream Soviet style of Communism. This intimidation from Moscow was not limited to only the Hungarian people. The same rhetoric was publicized in Poland, Czechoslovakia, Romania, and East Germany, not to mention all countries that were forced to become territories of the Soviet Union after WWII, such as Estonia, Latvia, and Lithuania.

People arrested during this era were treated with no respect for human rights. During interrogations, not only were they stripped from all their human dignity, they were frequently subjected to torture; beaten brutally in country where the government proudly announced: "our most important asset is the people." Eventually, these unfortunate people pleaded guilty for all the trumped-up charges manufactured by the Hungarian secret police (AVH) to stop the constant beatings and to bring to an end to their misery. Many government accusers and torturers were convinced that the majority of these people were just caught in the political turmoil and they were innocent of all the accusations imposed upon them. However, the officials and their goons were also afraid for themselves. They also were caught in a serious dilemma: either they did everything they were asked, even things that went against their own sense of right and wrong, or they might be end up in the same place as these unfortunate people did. Some of the "lucky ones" were given long jail sentences. Others, the unfortunate ones, were executed for their "crimes." The leaders of the Hungarian communists wanted to prove to their masters, the Soviets, that they were good comrades and ready for anything that the Communist leadership may ask of them to do for the greater cause of the communist political ideology.

A number of show trials also known as "window trials" were conducted in late 1940's and early 1950's. Interestingly enough, in the USA the "McCarthy era" also occurred during the same time. To fight against the Soviet Union and its allies, nicknamed the "cold war," the US government also conducted hearings to stamp out the threat of a Communist takeover of the country. People who were summoned to these hearings were forced to give out names of their friends, who may or may not have any connections the already outlawed Communist party. The people, who were accused of being Communists, lost their livelihood and their lives were made unbearable, but it never sunk to the level of the Communist bloc. The most famous trial was of Julius and Ethel Rosenberg. They were Jewish American communists who were executed in 1953 after they were found guilty of conspiracy to commit espionage. The charges were in relation to the passing information to the Soviet Union about the development of the atomic bomb. Their execution was the first of civilians for espionage in United States history. Even today, there is still controversy over their guilt or innocence.

One of the most famous trials in Hungary was the trial of László Rajk, the Interior Minister. In September 1949, he was arrested and later confessed to being an agent of many current and past enemies of the Soviet Union. Among them: Miklós Horthy, The Regent of Hungary until 1944, Leon Trotsky, opposition leader against Lenin, Josip Tito, President of Yugoslavia, a country that dared to break-away from Moscow and lastly, the Western imperialism. Within days of his arrest, his show trial started. László Rajk also admitted that he had taken part in a murder plot against Mátyás Rákosi and Ernő Gerő, the Minister of State. László Rajk was found guilty and he was executed within hours after the trial concluded. He was arrested for treason, which he did not commit. Years later in 1956, the government, still Communist, acknowledged his innocence and he was rehabilitated with a full pardon. An estimated 2,000 people were executed and an additional 100,000 more were imprisoned during the time when the new ruling Communists imposed their authoritarian rule on the Hungarian people. Under these circumstances, people were scared to say or to do anything that could be interpreted as reactionary behavior.

Ede was moved to the county jails in the city of Gyula. He was thrown into a damp, cold jail cell. The wooden bed was standing by the filthy wall; a heavily soiled sheet covered the bed with no pillows and no blankets. The cell was cold, no heat was provided during the cold winter, it was damp, it had a horrible smell, and it was dark since light could not get through the small dirty window facing the courtyard. He was shivering from the cold because they took away his warm coat and hat. Many thoughts were running through his head.

"What is going on with me?"

"What did I do to deserve this?"

"Why am I here?"

"Not long ago I survived the horrors of concentration camps, but at least then I knew why I was there." He felt guilty, frustrated, and simply scared for his life.

"What would happen to my family? What will happen to me?" He heard about the thousands of detainees who were arrested not because they did something horrible or illegal, but because someone for some reason made up charges indicating that these people were against the regime. The communist created and promoted a prejudice against most individuals who obtained good education in the past and anyone who accumulated wealth and owned lands and other properties in the past were labeled as "enemies of people." The phrase of "enemies of people," was a code word for enemies of the Communist ideology. This kind of "crime" cannot be tolerated. Of course, by now, the wealthy were penniless; intellectuals were working in menial jobs. Some of these people decided to join and became "believers," but the Communist leadership was suspicious of these people as a threat to their power.

Ede was well educated considering the standards of the 1920s. At this stage of his life Ede, had no money, had no power. He was struggling to survive after losing his job. Now, he felt sorry that he did not join those who had left Hungary after the war. Ede has never been a Zionist. Palestine was not his ideal place to settle permanently. He was considering a move to some western countries in Europe but most likely to the US. He always wanted to go to America. Unfortunately, something always prevented him from getting there.

On the other hand, he told himself:

"This setback will probably be nothing compared to the harsh conditions of Mauthausen and the suffering during the miserable war deep inside Russia. I survived all that, I will survive this, too."

The door opened abruptly. Two thugs, whom you would not like to meet at a dark alley at night, grabbed him by his arms and dragged him into another room. The room was dark with the exception of a dim light bulb hanging down from the ceiling creating a faded circle of light on the filthy floor below. They made Ede stand under the lighted area. While he was standing there, he felt the presence of someone, but did not see the person standing in the dark. After his eyes adjusted to the dark, Ede could see only the shadowy image of a man. He did not wear a uniform and Ede concluded that this guy must be a member of the secret police.

"So Mr. Kádár, how are you doing?" The man's voice had a gentle tone that Ede did not expect to hear under these circumstances. To start the interrogation, the interrogators usually tried to sound pleasant, hoping to skip the unpleasantness of the interrogation and get a quick confession, which would result in them going home early.

"I am well," Ede replied slowly, "but, I have been better."

"Do you have any idea why are you here?" the voice continued. Now the voice sounded familiar.

"I do not," he quickly replied.

"You should."

"Why don't you tell me?" This time Ede took his time to reply. Stopped for a few seconds and slowly continued. "I know you will and I do not have to guess."

One of the goons hit his face hard with his fist and shouted at him:

"Shut up you dirty Jew; you must address the Comrade with respect!" Ede had flashbacks from his miserable past, but he had never expected this kind of talk from a government official. Well, he was wrong. A Jew was a Jew in the eyes of an anti-Semite, no matter where they are or whom they serve. Ede kept quiet, did not respond. The same goon hit him again.

"Are you deaf? The Captain asked you a question!" The man shouted again like a vicious animal. Ede still would not say a word. He knew these kinds of people; no matter what answer he gave, they would continue their "script" anyway. The purpose of the interrogation was to try to break the inmate so he confessed to the predetermined crimes "committed." A few more hits to his face, to his body and few more unarticulated shouts by these ruthless tools of horror, but without getting any reaction from Ede. His nose and his upper lips were bleeding. Finally, the captain's voice interrupted and gave his instruction with authority:

"Stop, let him speak freely. Take his handcuff off." He offered a clean handkerchief to wipe the blood. Ede took it and tried to clean his wounds. Ede still kept quite.

"Listen, Mr. Kádár," the voice continued with disappointment. "Sit down and let us talk like civilized people!" It was an oxymoron, civilized communist people!

Ede sat down on the chair supplied to him by one of the men. His face and his body were hurting, but considering, he felt reasonably well. His hunger was hurting him even more than the few slaps on his face. The Captain also sat down and revealed his face. Ede recognized him. Before the Communist had taken over, he was a low-level administrator in the county government. He had never amounted to anything before. People suspected him to be a communist sympathizer before the Communists came to power, but his allegiance had never been confirmed until now.

"OK, Mr. Kocsis," Ede started speak. "What do you want from me? I am not a criminal. As far as I know, I have not done anything against you or anyone else in your circle. I did not hurt anyone nor did I steal anything." Ede paused and took a deep breath. "Why are you treating me like this?" Ede was surprised by the calmness in his voice. Certainly, Ede felt superior to this person. As far as Ede was concerned, he was still an insignificant nobody.

"I am sure you are aware, Comrade Kádár, that we wanted you to join us, the new government chosen by the working class people, and we wanted you to help us as an experienced leader or as an experienced administrator. We, the new Communist leadership, need your expertise to govern the people." Comrade Kocsis has spoken.

"I am sure you too, Mr. Kocsis, knew about my decision to stay away from politics," Ede said to him calmly. "I do not want any power. I have a lovely wife, I have a new son whom I adore, and want to raise him to be an honest member of society. That is all I want, nothing else."

Comrade Kocsis started to shout something obscene that Ede could not quite understood and he dashed out from the interrogation room. Ede was escorted back to a different cell with eight other prisoners. Ede did not know any of these people.

His trips to the interrogation room became a daily event, but they never hit him again. A few minutes of shouting, asking useless questions, and getting useless answers in return were the daily program. No end was in sight.

The prisoners were fed once a day with some terrible, indescribable food. Ede in his mind kept comparing the current treatment to Mauthausen. Of course, his treatment could not be compared to the horrors of a concentration camp; but these comparisons made his life in prison more bearable. Days passed without anything-important happening and without knowing what the future would bring.

§ § § § § §

The vice-president of the Jewish community of Békéscsaba, Izsak Lebovitz, finally decided to try to do something to help Ede. Everyone in the community knew that Ede had a brother, Arthur, who had already established himself as a "devout" communist. They were hoping that Arthur might be able to help to free his brother. However, Mr. Lebovitz knew that he had to be careful. It was widely known that brothers would turn against brothers just to save their own skins. In any case, he decided to take a trip to Kisvárda and talk to Arthur in person.

Mr. Lebovitz did not know where Arthur lived, so he went to the synagogue that was standing in the center of the town of Kisvárda. As was customary, the residence of the local Rabbi was in the courtyard of the synagogue. He introduced himself to the Rabbi and inquired about Ede's brother. The Rabbi, who happened to be the brother-in-law of Ede and Arthur, told him that Arthur is a good man and he is not like most Communists. He indeed held a high position in the Communist Party. The Rabbi also warned Mr. Lebovitz that Arthur might not be willing to risk his position to help his own brother. Nevertheless, if Mr. Lebovitz wanted to talk to Arthur, he probably would not have any problems. The Rabbi showed his guest the way to Arthur's house and rushed back to his own house, before anyone spotted him with the stranger.

The ten-minute walk seemed much longer to Mr. Lebovitz. Now, he was a little bit scared but he was determined to do what needed to be done. Besides, he was the one who wanted to do this, so let it be. Arthur lived in a nice house on a quiet street in Kisvárda. He peeked through the gate and a well-kept courtyard, with beautiful flowers in various flowerbeds scattered all around the yard was revealed. A young woman was sitting by a table under a large tree that provided soothing relief from the hot sun. He knocked on the gate. He got startled when a large black dog run towards him, but since the gate was locked Mr. Lebovitz had nothing to fear. The dog kept barking even after the young women tried to silence him.

"Oh, shut up Betyár," he heard the lovely voice of the young woman try to calm down the dog. Of course, as dogs usually do, he did not budge.

"Can I help you?" she asked Mr. Lebovitz.

"Good day. My name is Mr. Lebovitz. I would like to talk to Arthur Kádár."

"Please come in, Arthur is in his study." She escorted him inside the house.

"My name is Izsak Lebovitz and I am from Békéscsaba," he started nervously. "Your brother is in trouble, he was arrested a few months ago, and we have not heard anything from him since."

"Do you know why was he taken away?" Arthur asked.

"We truly do not know for sure. We do not know where he is at this moment. The only thing we heard was that he was charged with gun possession. We really do not know anything else! Do you think you could help him?" Izsak was so nervous. He was blurting out words not realizing that he kept repeating himself. He could not stop talking. Finally, Arthur interrupted him,

"I am glad you came to let me know. I did not know or hear anything about his arrest. Please, go home and do not talk to anyone about our meeting. Do not mention anything, even to Helen, about this." He stopped for a moment and after taking a deep breath, slowly he continued:

"I will see if I can do anything. You should know these are dangerous times, you do not want yourself or any of us to get into any trouble!"

Izsak did not even remember leaving Arthur's house. He went directly to the train station and waited for hours until the next train finally came. It was well after midnight by the time he got home to Békéscsaba. He told his wife about the trip and the warning against telling anyone else about it. They were hoping that everything would turn for the better.

§ § § § § §

His fellow prisoners were reluctant to talk to him. In the beginning, Ede did not understand the reason he was being shunned. There was another prisoner, who kept offering cigarettes to him and to the others. Cigarettes were important for the prisoners because most of them were heavy smokers and cigarettes were not provided. To deny cigarettes to a smoker was cruel punishment, but this was not as bad as the treatment by the prison guards. He took the cigarettes offered by this man in the beginning, but after awhile Ede realized that, the guy offering the cigarettes was a mole. It was a common practice to plant a mole to gain information from the prisoners. It took Ede some time to stop talking to this man.

Every day prisoners were taken in and out from their cells. Some returned and some of them disappeared. Most inmates worried about their own fate, they did not care about what happened to the others. Not the mole, when a new prisoner arrived, this person was the first to great him. Most knew about the mole; they would not speak to him or took his cigarettes. After a while, Ede realized that most of his roommates believed that he was one of the moles. Unlike most others in the cell, he kept coming back without any visible beating marks on him; he had at least one trait of a mole. Ede, who could not stop talking all his life, was the kind of person who kept conversations alive with his interesting stories, became depressed and quiet. Most of the time, he was laying on his back daydreaming about his past life.

§§§§§§

He was born during an era when some of the greatest Hungarian Jewish minds became well known all over the world for their accomplishments. John von Neumann was one of the greatest mathematicians that ever lived and he was considered the father of the computer. He, along with Leo Szilárd, Edward Teller, and Eugene Wigner helped to develop the atom bomb. The artistry of photographers André Kertész and Robert Capa become known throughout the world. Alexander Korda and Michael Curtiz became world-renowned film producers and directors. Arthur Koesler became a powerful author and there were many others.

When Ede was growing up, he did not know or hear about these people. He grew up in Kisvárda, a small town in the northeast of Hungary. He did not have the chance to further his education beyond high school. In 1920, the first anti-Semite laws in Europe were introduced in Hungary called "Numerous Clausus" limiting Jewish enrollments into universities. In his immediate family, only one of his older brothers was able to attend higher education and he became a physician. In those days however, Ede was considered a well-educated man by earning a special high-school degree from the Civil Gymnasium (Polgári). Like many of his contemporaries, he was drafted into the military service after high school. Most Jewish laws were not yet enacted to depress the lives of Jews in the early 1920s. In the military, he had found himself. He enjoyed his military days so much, that he could not stop talking about his "glorious days" of serving in the army. After completed his basic training, Ede was assigned to the Hussar (Cavalier) regiment and became a Lieutenant. He was tall, dark, and handsome wearing his colorful Hussar uniform and made women's heads turn wherever he appeared. No question about it, he was well aware of his power, his sex appeal and used it to his advantage. He was a real ladies man and broke many young women's hearts.

Ede started to smile when he got to this point in his daydream remembering a funny incident that he survived and could talk about ever since. Even his wife, Helen, was making jokes about this incident labeled "waving the flag."

He frequently visited the main street of the town where he was stationed at one point. On the main street in most towns and cities, people were walking with friends and family to relax or visiting shops to purchase various things. He kept noticing a gorgeous young woman with beautiful red hair and a curvaceous figure. Redheads were one of his weaknesses (along with brunettes and blonds.) He started to inquire about her, especially after he noticed that when their eyes met for a second, she had a flirting little smile on her beautifully shapely face.

"Forget about her, she is the wife of the police chief, who is about 190 centimeter tall and carries a gun," people warned him. Well, this kind of warning made the challenge even more exciting.

"I will have her, you can bet on it!" he told his friends. Well Ede lost this bet, kind of! Ede managed to find the home of this beauty, and like a secret agent, he kept his eye on the house. Her husband had a daily routine: after finishing his lunch at home, he would leave the house and go back to work at precisely 12:45 PM and usually would not return home until finishing his work at about 5:00 PM, enough time for an affair. Remember the world "usually."

It was a hot summer day when Ede finally decided to make his move. Most people stayed inside their houses trying to escape the summer heat. He knocked on the front door and the woman of his desires opened the door. She was wearing a loose cotton summer dress with buttons on the front. Obviously, she was hot, a couple of the top buttons of her dress were unbuttoned, revealing the outlines of her firm breasts, and these beauties were practically bursting out from her dress. His eyes like laser beams were immediately scanning this delicious view, with anticipation for more than just a view to come. She was not expecting any visitors at this time of the day. She could not believe her eyes seeing Ede standing and staring by her unexpectedly.

"My husband is not home," she shyly mumbled, but shouting with excitement in her mind and in her eyes. "HE IS HERE! What am I going to do?" Her own thoughts made her blush and this made her even more desirable for Ede. "I know," replied Ede coyly. "That is why I am here." She was not one of the brightest women in the world, but quickly she realized, it is happening, what she had been yearning for one day to take place. She grabbed Ede's arm.

"Please get in before any of the neighbors see you," she nervously yelled, covering her shapely mouth, realizing that her reaction could draw even more attention to the situation.

They entered the bedroom. The shades were drawn to shield the heat from outside, giving a mysterious darkness to the room's atmosphere. Passion made the hot stuffy air seem even hotter. She was nervous, having never been in this situation before. She had no idea how to precede, what she should do next. She was standing there and waiting for the next moment with great anticipation. Ede, on the other hand, lived for these moments. This was a situation when words were completely unnecessary. Their bodies knew exactly what to do, and of course, Ede's experience helped to move things along. He put his arm around her tiny waist; their lips stuck together so long it seemed as if they could never come apart. The hot air and their passion made both of their bodies sweat. Then, slowly Ede started to undo all the buttons on her dress. She pulled away as if she got scared. However, that was not the case. She let her dress fall down revealing one of God's most beautiful creations. She was completely naked. Ede just realized, he was still fully clothed, and as quickly as humanly possible, he shed all his clothes and the two passionate bodies embraced again.

All of a sudden, they both froze. Someone had opened the front door. You may have guessed right, the husband unexpectedly came home, what a shame! What a loss!

"O my god," the girl whispered, "my husband is home!" Ede knew, but almost forgot that the husband was a policeman, he carried a gun, and he was a big strong fellow, much bigger than Ede. He had no choice. He better get out fast or…but how he could he get out, when the husband was blocking the front door? He panicked, with no time to dress, he grabbed his underwear, not realizing the need for any other garments, and jumped out the window stark naked. Ede was smiling, when he got to this part of his daydream. He still remembers the expressions on people's faces seeing a completely naked man running down on their normally uneventful street, waiving his underpants like a flag. He became a legend in this small town. Nice memories, but he had to come back from his dreams and face the awful reality: he was lying on filthy bed in a dirty prison cell.

§ § § § § §

Other friends of Ede in Békéscsaba also started to make inquiries. Béla Bánki, like Arthur, had made it big with the Communists. He was also approachable, but everyone in the Jewish community was afraid to talk to Béla. Uncle Yayli, with his long beard was widely known in Békéscsaba by Jews and non-Jews alike. He was the collector of dues for the Jewish congregation. He frequently visited active and not so active congregants. He figured that he would be the best person to approach Béla. There were other Jews living in the apartment house where Béla had his residence, thus no one would be suspicious if visited Béla. Uncle Yayli knocked on the door and Béla's wife was surprised to see him in her doorway. She let everybody's Uncle Yayli come into the apartment.

"Is your husband home?" he asked.

"No, he is at work." she skittishly answered. "Can I help you with something?" she offered.

"Yes, you may be able to. You know Ede Kádár; he is my friend and far as I know, he is your husband's good friend, too. He was arrested a few months ago. I wanted to ask your husband if he might know something about his whereabouts. I wanted to ask him if he could help our friend." All of a sudden, Edna's face became white as a sheet. She was scared this was a dangerous request.

"Please go away before you got us into trouble!" she shouted with a subdued voice. She pushed Uncle Yayli out the apartment and slammed the door in his face.

§ § § § §

It was a hot summer day. Every time Ede was going to the interrogation room, he had a chance to peek out through one of the dirty windows in the hallway. The sky was beautifully blue, interrupted only by tiny spots of white fluffy clouds. It felt hot, but he no longer had any feelings for life's little pleasures like this. He was depressed and did not see or care about anything. He started to believe that there was no future for him. The daily "interrogations" were meaningless and useless. This shenanigan was going nowhere and his interrogators were starting to get tired of seeing him and talking to him without any results. This day, however, was different. When the guard came for him, he took Ede into a different room: a bathroom. They gave him a towel and soap. The bathtub was filled with nice soothing warm water. This was the first time he had a bath for months. It felt so good.

"Now I can die clean," he was wondering. He finished his bath and shaved off his overgrown beard. The guard gave him some clean underwear, pants, and a shirt. He looked pale, but presentable. After he finished, he was escorted into an office where he found Béla sitting behind a desk.

"Hi, Ede," greeted him cheerfully. "We need to talk before you go home."

"How did you get here? What are you doing here? Did you say I could go home?" Ede kept asking him.

"I know you are extremely tired, frustrated, and angry." Béla was ignoring Ede's questions. "Listen to me Ede, after you have gone home please try to forget everything about the past few months. I know, it will be hard to resist talking about it, but you must do what I am telling you for your own sake, for my sake, for our families' sakes." Béla stopped for a moment to emphasize the seriousness of this moment.

"Please, in the future do not talk about what happened to you during the last 8 months and especially do not ever mention our conversation to anyone. I promise to you that you and your family will be all right."

"Again, I have to ask you, please do not mention to anyone about me and everything we spoke of today!" Béla told Ede all this with a very worried expression on his face. They did not have to say anything more; they both could imagine all the troubles they may face in the future if this conversation would ever get out.

Ede kept his word and spoke about his time in jail, about his treatment by the sadistic guards and about this conversation with Béla until the end of his life.

After the discussion, the guard escorted him to the train station, bought him a ticket, and put him on the train home to Békéscsaba.

TOP—EDE AND LASZLO, 1947
BOTTOM—MRS. HAJDU AND LASZLO, 1947

HELEN AND LASZLO, 1948

TOP—HELEN AND LASZLO, 1947
BOTTOM—THE KADAR FAMILY, 1948

TOP—VILLA'S DECAYING STYLISH TERRACE, 2011
BOTTOM—TREFORT ST VILLA IN BÉKÉSCSABA, 2011

9

hard, trying years

It was almost eight months since Ede had been taken away. It was not easy for Helen to be alone with Lacika. She had gotten used to the nice comfortable life that Ede was able to provide for her until now. On the other hand, Helen made new friends in Békéscsaba, the kind of friends she never had before. When she was young, she connected only with people who were either her relatives or the relatives of relatives. She never was close to these people. Most of her immediate family and friends perished during the Holocaust. She also had acquaintances like her customers or neighbors from the Jewish community. Nevertheless, with the exception of her family she was living with in Mátészalka, she never developed any true friendships with anyone.

After moving to Békéscsaba, she felt lost and many times felt lonely. The arrival of Lacika provided a great uplifting effect on her mood and outlook on life. She felt she had a reason and purpose to be alive. Her daily life was completely encircled by providing the best care for her husband and for her child. Having a child around gave her a chance to meet other mothers and she made a few friends of her own. She started to have a "social life," a new life that she enjoyed.

She was a great cook. She made simple but delicious food and wonderful cakes and cookies. Her health, unfortunately, was not so great. She was constantly worried about what would happen to her son, if god-forbid, she would die. She never expected, or ever imagined the possibility of anything happening to Ede. After the few comfortable years in Békéscsaba, this tragedy brought back all her past insecurities. Because her health, she knew she could not hold down a regular job. She was contemplating starting to make custom-made girdles and bras again, but the communist government would never allow her to open up a salon. Besides, how could she take care of a small child and run a business together? People more or less kept away from her. Even her newly found friends were afraid to visit her with any regular frequency. Helen was alone and depressed. Lacika was the only thing that kept her going.

Financially, she was able to manage for the time being. As the Director of Displaced Properties, Ede had earned a good salary and had been able to save some money. Helen was lucky because during the invasion of their house, the goons did not find their hidden saved money.

§ § § § § §

After the war, most people would not trust banks. During those uncertain times, one would never know what the next day might bring. Like many others, especially Jewish people, the Kádár family kept their money hidden in mattresses and other "safe" places definitely not in any banks. What happened to Ede proved their concern. If their money had been deposited in a bank, the government would have confiscated it. The money helped Helen a great deal during the long eight months without Ede.

Helen was managing her money well, but as time went on, she was more and more concerned about her future. She had no idea of her husband's whereabouts or his fate in the brutal hands of the communists. She started to receive some financial help from the Jewish community, which helped to reduce her anxiety a little bit. Uncle Yayli and his wife never stopped caring for her. This old Hassidic Jew did not care about, or maybe did not realize, the potential danger he may face by helping an "enemy of the State." As a religious Jew, he felt that he had a moral obligation to be there any time his fellow Jews needed him. Uncle Yayli was right the government completely ignored him. He proved to be a real friend and the two family's friendship lasted for the rest of their lives and spread two continents.

§ § § § § §

It was a hot summer day in mid August 1949. On this lazy, hot summer afternoon, Helen was relaxing on the terrace and reading a book. She liked to sit on this beautiful terrace. Two doors were leading into the house. One of the doors was no longer in use ever since the rest of the house was taken away. A medical office moved into the vacated part of the house and the patients and the medical personnel were using only the main entrance on the front. The terrace remained a private area for the Kádár family. The other door was the entrance to their apartment. The terrace was overlooking the backyard with hand-carved stone columns forming a line of curved columns. The top of the columns were connected by a continuous long flowerpot in which petunias and other summer flowers were in full bloom and provided visual beauty and an aromatic scent like a French perfume. The floor was covered by colorful Italian tiles. The afternoon sun had already moved over to the other side of the house so the house provided comfortable shade on the terrace. Lacika was playing somewhere in the backyard.

The entertaining book that Helen was reading kept her so deeply concentrated that she lost touch with her surroundings. Suddenly, she felt a gentle kiss on her neck. Since she had not heard anyone coming, she got surprised and let out a frightened scream. She jumped up from her chair and started to weep, but the tears coming from her eyes were the tears of happiness. Ede was standing front of her, a bit fragile, a bit skinny, but very much alive. Words were unnecessary; their emotions were speaking for themselves.

"Lacika where are you?" Helen yelled with a tremble in her voice. "Come here and see who is here!"

Eight months was an awful long time in a small child's life. Lacika was not sure whom this man was holding onto his mother. The eight months of suffering had put its mark on Ede. He seemed to be aged and his salt-and-peppery hair was noticeably lighter. He lost a great deal of weight and looked a little bit pale. Other than that, he seemed to be in good health.

"Don't you recognize your father?" Helen said. Lacika let out a big scream and run to embrace Ede and he would not let him go. Lacika was crying, but he had no idea why he was crying, after all, his mother was crying, too. On the other hand, crying felt good. Maybe he did not realize until now how much he had missed his father, and now it felt good to have the secure feeling that his father was again here for him.

"Are you hungry?" Helen's wifely instincts come to surface. "I am not sure if I have any dinner for you," she continued.

"I could use some food," Ede replied, "but no rush. Let me hold you a bit longer. I missed you so much." They talked for a long time not realizing that the sun already descended, the evening had come, and the courtyard was dark.

They went inside the house to eat something. As in most Hungarian households in those days, one could always find something to eat.

They had the customary light supper consisting buttered fresh bread along with some soft cheeses and salad consisting of green pepper, tomato and radishes. Lacika drank hot cocoa and the grownups had tea to wash all this down. In the first time in eight months, the couple was sleeping next to each other, embracing and relaxing. Ede was happy to be with his wife and he could finally sleep in his comfortable bed again.

The next morning Ede went to the synagogue for the Morning Prayer to give thanks to G-d for his safe return. The people were happy to see him back. After the service was over, some sat down with Ede and asked him if he has any plans for the future, what would he do to make a living? At this stage, Ede had no clue, but he was assuring them he would figure out something soon. He was well aware that for an observant Jew it was difficult to find any job where the Shabbat could be observed. In those days, the five-day workweek was not the norm. Ede would not work on Saturdays.

§ § § § § §

By now, you the reader know that Ede was a survivor. After the war was over, many American Jews felt obligated to help their fellow European Jews. They tried to find any surviving relatives, especially relatives in Easter European countries, where the iron grip of the Soviet Union kept people in an even worse economic situation than their Western neighbors did. Many families were happy to receive care packages from overseas. These packages contained mostly clothing with occasional nonperishable foodstuff like chocolates and canned goods.

Uncle Eugene was a grand uncle of Helen, living in New York since 1914. Eugene somehow contacted Helen, and sent many packages over the years. In one of these packages, he sent a couple of leather belts made of small pieces of leather chained together creating an unusual looking belt. Most men wore belts except for those who opted for the more traditional German suspenders (Hosenträger) Ede was among the latter group. Nevertheless, this piece of accessory gave Ede the idea that provided his employment for many years to come.

§ § § § § §

Hungary has a long history of producing quality shoes and other leather goods. Logic would dictate that after the leather was cut to create the desired products, leftover pieces could not be used for anything else useful. These leftover pieces were thrown away as useless material. These were hard years. Shortages of materials were the heart of the economic problems of the Communist post-war economy. He prepared a proposal to utilize these leather remnants to produce useful and badly needed products. The proposal described a small-scale manufacturing effort producing accessories such leather belts and suspenders, briefcases and other light leather items. These items turned out to be in short supply.

To create a set of prototypes, Ede hired a blacksmith to forge a few iron cast formats (metal stamps) with different shapes. Then Ede obtained a strong wooden hammer and a large timber with one end smoothed down to create a flat surface. He got some leftover leathers from a local shoemaker and he was ready to create.

He placed a piece of leather on the flat surface of the timber and placed one of the iron formats with the sharp end down. With his other hand, using the wooden hammer, he whacked the iron. The form cut through the leather creating a perfectly shaped piece of leather. He examined the piece and he was happy with his first attempt. He kept up the pace and created many more pieces.

To produce a belt was relatively easy. The pieces he created for this purpose looked like a fat number 8. He placed a belt buckle on the middle skinny part of the 8 and then folded the leather piece in half, aligning the two holes on top of each other. Next, he threaded the next piece through the hole and then folding it in half as he done with the first piece. He continued the threading until the desired length of the belt been reached. At the end, he cut a longer piece of leather by hand. After, he threaded that piece as the last piece, folded it, and glued it. He punched several small holes into this piece for the prong of the belt buckle. The belt was completed and it looked nice.

Ede's next move was to figure out how to construct a briefcase. He created pieces that looked like an even-sided triangle. He laid old newspaper pages flat on the table and with a brush smeared some glue on one side. Carefully, he placed a row of triangles lining them along the top of the paper, neatly forming a straight line of triangles. The next line was created by placing the triangle pieces in the opposite direction, so their pointy part faced up, overlaying the edges of two existing pieces. He laid the next row by placing the triangles in the same direction as the first row was and he careful put them on the top of the bottom part of the previous rows. Two pieces of leather now formed a rhombus like shape. He continued doing this until the newspaper page was completely filled. The creation had some kind of rhythmical feel to it due to the way the triangles were aligned.

He waited until his creation was completely dried and picked up the piece, but it seemed somewhat fragile. He turned it over and glued a piece of blue cloth on the back that later doubled as the lining of the briefcase. When he was done, he walked over to Mr. Schwartz, the local shoemaker, who had a sewing machine for leather goods. Mr. Schwartz carefully sewed together each piece along their edges. The final product looked sturdy. The final phase of the assembly was to cut these panels into smaller pieces. Finally, these parts were sewn together to form a briefcase, he also added a handle and lock. After the first briefcase was completed, they both agreed that it looked like a nice product. Their new creation looked different from a normal briefcase, but Ede felt confident that people would buy these products if the price were right.

Of course, Ede was not done yet. He had to sell his idea to someone, but the question was to whom? He needed a job fast. He needed to find consumers for his product, soon.

§ § § § § §

The communist terror was in full force. The government made its business to keep every individual under surveillance. Intrusions into the private lives of people were nonstop, boundless, and limitless. Everyone had to carry a passport-like identification booklet called "personal identification," containing the usual demographics like name, birth date, and place of residence. Employers must register every employee's current work location with starting and ending date of employment, this ID would contain the entire work history of the owner. The current and past residences were also carefully recorded in this ID booklet by the local police. Failure to register changes was punishable by law. People were wondering why bother with the ID, the police would know about the changes anyway. The police could stop anyone, at any time of the day or night, without any reason to check the individual's ID. If this ID was not updated properly, the person could be arrested. If there was no current valid residence listed, the person could be arrested. If there were no current employment listed, the person could be arrested.

The Communist ideology states that everyone must work. Since there were no longer rich people around anymore, we know that the Communists had taken care of rich people. People need to work and earn their money from a job, because this was the only way to pay for food, shelter, and any other things that a person may need to survive. How could anyone survive without earning a regular income? If one did not work, then he or she must be a criminal. Unlike in a democratic society, the rule of the land was "one was guilty until proven innocent." Ede had already experienced this philosophy on his own skin. His ID stated that he was recently released from jail and currently not employed. He had to find a steady source of income soon, before he gets himself into trouble again.

Ede found out that his friend, Mr. Katz had become the manager of his own "factory," after the Communists nationalized it. The tiny factory, employing less than 30 people, was located in a small town about 20 km away from Békéscsaba. It was producing simple primitive looking products like gloves, aprons, hats, etc. Even though the Communists took away his factory, he remained as a manager. Sometimes this kind of arrangement was tolerated, since some of the government-controlled factories had to have qualified managers to produce badly needed basic products and ex-owners were happy to oblige; at least they had jobs and did not end up in labor camps, as many non-desired "capitalists" did. Ede went to see Jenő to introduce his new business idea.

"Hello Jenő. How have you been doing lately?" greeted him, when Ede arrived to the factory.

"It is nice to see you and I am glad to see you so well!" Jenő replied with a happy smile on his face. There were a numbers of people around and they had to resort to small talk, one never knows who was listening…

§ § § § § §

Even though on paper Mr. Katz was in charge, he was not really in charge. The Communists did not trust anyone. Many times, they did not even trust some of their own. In most institutions, the true power was entrusted to a devout Communist, he or she was appointed by the Communist Party. These people most likely did not have formal education nor had any practical knowledge about running a factory. Any organization: offices, farms, factories, movies, hotels, public swimming pools, churches, and synagogues were infiltrated with government moles; the larger the organization, the more moles were planted. Most of the moles may not even have been aware of the existence of other moles within the same workplace.

Unless one lived during this time in Hungary, or any other satellite countries, one might not be able to understand life under communism.

Living in a free society, one could not imagine existing this way. Most of the time, people knew or suspected who were the moles, but one can never be completely sure, therefore most people would not discuss anything private when other people were around. Parents were afraid of their own children. We all know, children do tell the truth. Dishonesty was a learned behavior. The Communists also signed up for this theory. In schools kid were asked well-directed and phrased questions and too many times the authorities arrested parents formulating from indictments based upon the answers of their own children.

The Communists adapted the ideology called "Dictatorship of the Proletariat" by Karl Marx. The struggle between classes, according to Marx, has to come to the path of taking over the power from the upper classes (bourgeoisie) and establish the power of the working men (Proletariat), who must organize itself as the ruling class. The government established in Hungary in 1948 declared this movement as the revolution of the Proletariat. To build their strength, the communists used many techniques to control the general population. The true authority was entrusted by the Communist Party to their most faithful and trustworthy members. These low-level bureaucrats were recruited mostly from uneducated people who could not think for themselves, but they were able to absorb the entire demagogy of Communism and become enthused and invigorated by this new way of life. These people had been given preferential treatment for their jobs and other benefits that the rest of the population might not be able to obtain. Even in their dreams, these people could not imagine to reach this kind of social level for themselves without the help of the ruling Communists.

§ § § § § §

"Let us go to my office Ede," Mr. Katz said. They went into his small office located near to the entrance of the factory. They hoped for a little more privacy in there, but one may never know for sure.

"Jenő, you do not have to worry. I came to propose a legal business venture." Ede started his conversation and showed him the prototypes he made. Jenő was impressed.

"These are really good, how do you plan to produce these?" Jenő asked. "I do not have any manufacturing capabilities for these kinds of products."

"We will not need you to produce these."

"Where would you get materials? How would you sell them? Who and where would you make these products?" Jenő kept asking Ede with a great deal of interest in his voice.

"My idea is as follows: We will obtain a contract from your superiors to open up a satellite factory in Békéscsaba, and I will take care of the rest. As you know, there are many religious Jews in Békéscsaba and they would not work on Saturdays. Because this restriction these people have problems finding jobs. This idea would help them making a decent living to support their family."

"How about the Seven-day-Adventist, they also have problem working on Saturday." Jenő suggested. "This group of people may be willing to join and their existence would help the argument for the new factory."

"This is a good idea Jenő," Ede replied. "I will approach them. Please do not talk to anyone about the work free Saturdays. We will bring this question up only if we already have the approval for the factory."

The two discussed Ede's plan in more details and they both agreed that the idea might be workable. The first hurdle was obtaining the go-a-head from his bosses in Budapest. The approval for a satellite factory would be easier to get from Budapest than getting an approval from the bureaucrats in the regional Communist government to allow working on Sundays instead of Saturdays. The two made a promise to start working on their individual plans as soon as possible and hoped that both of them could report success soon. As we know, the timing was extremely crucial for Ede. The next day Ede, took a train to the city of Szeged to visit a well-known large shoe factory.

§ § § § § §

Szeged was a city with a population of over 100,000 and in 1940's it was one of the largest cities in Hungary. This city was best known for its many universities educating a new generation of medical doctors, engineers and teachers. The city was considered the regional cultural center of south Hungary with active theaters producing plays and even classical operas and concerts. The flood of 1879 by Hungary's second largest river, Tisza, almost destroyed the entire city. The following few years with the encouragement of Franz Joseph I, Hungarian-Austrian emperor, from the ruins a modern city was created. The newly built avenues and boulevards imitated the layout of the city of Paris and the beauty of the newly rebuilt Szeged competed with Budapest. For some, Szeged was considered the most beautiful city in Hungary after Budapest.

§ § § § § §

This time Ede was not interested in the city's sites, he wanted to convince the leadership of the South Hungarian Shoes Factory (Dél Magyar Cipő Gyár) to sell their leather remnants to his proposed "Waste Processing Company." Prior to visiting, he called the production manager of the factory and described his plans in some detail. The manager invited Ede to discuss his proposal in person in front of his superiors. The meeting lasted less than a half hour and they agreed. Ede could not believe how easy it was. The leadership of the factory was happy to find a way to get rid of and be paid for their entire "throw away" useless materials. One problem was solved!

§ § § § § §

In the Communist economic system, everything was centrally controlled. The Communist economists in those days did not believe in the law of supply and demand model for running their economical system. The main controlling force for production and distribution of goods was politically motivated. Corruption was out of control. There were shortages of goods and new products were badly needed, but officially, no one would dare to acknowledge any of these shortages and production issues. Starting in 1947, the economic system of Hungary was mirroring the Soviet model.

At first, there was a three-year economic plan followed by a succession of five-year plans. The goals of these ambitious plans were to increase the production of goods, both industrial and farming, to a level that would surpass the production levels of the pre-World War II era. The chronic shortages of natural resources did not stop the bureaucrats of the Communist leadership to plan for unrealistic production levels. By 1949, the nationalization of banks, factories, mines, commerce, at both wholesale and retail level, was completed. After the communist takeover, many farmers, probably for the first time in their lives, were given farmlands of their own, to bribe these people into supporting the communists. Shortly after the people received their land, the government decided to create collective farms, using the Soviet kolkhoz as a model. The consolidation of the majority of small farms into collective farms was completed by forcing all small landowners to "volunteer" their newly obtained land to the collective farm system.

The central government hierarchy was in complete control of all production and distribution of goods. On the bottom of the hierarchy was the individual factory leadership, who lost all their autonomy. Their responsibilities were limited to fulfilling the will of their superiors. These five-year plans contained instructions down to each individual employee and determined who, when, from what, and how much each individual needed to produce. The Soviet Union leadership and their economists developed a communist worldview theorizing that it was possible to make the most efficient use of resources in this manner. In this new order, decisions were not driven by profitability, and as a result, certain industry segments were targeted for growth and others were neglected. Work-competitions were encouraged and these competitions were based on producing as many of these products as humanly possible and completely ignoring quality and usability as a measurement of success. In addition, it was expected from a good Communist to volunteer some of his or her time to perform additional work as a token of appreciation for all the "great achievements" that the Communist Ideology brought for the common working people. Unfortunately, for the Hungarian people, most of the useful goods produced served the Soviet market, creating huge shortages in Hungary.

The emergence of the cold war and the perceived threat of an actual war, provided the government a rationale to force the "ideological re-education" of the population and giving a "reasonable" cause for the poor economic conditions, in other words all the hardships of the Hungarian people was caused by the western capitalists and imperialists.

The supplies of consumer goods were centrally controlled from Budapest. Each individual retail store would get a disbursement of goods from one of the assigned suppliers, controlled by a single bureaucrat sitting in a Budapest central office. The powers of these petty bureaucrats were coming from their party affiliation only. These individuals, many times uneducated bureaucrats, could not differentiate between goods that the general populations badly needed or products that could not be sold because nobody would want or needed them.

Ede had to find just one bureaucrat who would be willing to risk a decision to support his effort. He had to find only one well-positioned bureaucrat who would buy and distribute his proposed products to one of the government-controlled stores like the "State Department Store" (Állami Áruház) and Ede would succeed in his endeavor. A branch of the "State Department Store" was located in most major cities and towns throughout Hungary. This mission was probably the most difficult job, because he had to rely on people who could not be trusted. The challenge for Ede was to find a person who could and would help, but would not turn against Ede. He knew many of these bureaucrats could be bribed, but it was difficult to gauge who was approachable or who was a "true believer." Approaching the wrong person could cause serious problems for Ede.

Well, Ede was hoping that someone in the Jewish Community in
Budapest had connections and might introduce Ede to a high-level
official who was not a "true believer." Ede was hoping to find someone, who may know somebody else, who might be able to direct
him to the right bureaucrat. The right connection was everything.
By the end of the day, Ede had his buyer. His name was Dr. Gyula
Kiss, the chairman of the local Communist Party at the Budapest
Headquarter of State Department Store. He was a political appoin-
tee. He was willing to do almost anything for the right price. Ede
met him in a café. It was always advisable to meet in a neutral public place; one never knew who was listening. They agreed to his fees
and he promised to arrange all the necessary steps (bureaucratic and
administrative) needed to move forward. It looked liked the second
problem was solved, or at least it was heading in the right direction!

§ § § § § §

You, the reader, may not be knowledgeable of the Hungarian history under communist rule, please note the following facts: The
Communist leadership despised and discouraged any religious practices and conducts. They openly "preached" that all religions were
created for the control and exploitation of uneducated people. You
could note a very interesting thing: the Communist leadership
employed exactly the same basic philosophy. It was true that uneducated people, most likely than not, would accept anything that an
"educated" person, especially a person with authority such as a
priest, a government official, a communist party leader, would tell
them, especially because these uneducated people would not have a
way to invalidate the claims of these people in charge.

A new constitution was created in 1949. One of the most interesting previsions in this totally Communist constitution states: "The
Hungarian People's Republic insures the citizens' freedom of conscience and the right of the free practice of any religion." (54. § (1)
A Magyar Népköztársaság biztosítja a polgárok lelkiismereti
szabadságát és a vallás szabad gyakorlásának jogát.)

§ § § § § §

Let me tell you something, after all that happened to him, Ede
sure had guts. Since the new constitution included the right of practicing religion, Ede was encouraged to fight for his people, for himself, and for his family. Based upon this law, he made sure that
Lacika never attended elementary school on Saturdays and any Jew-

ish holidays and Ede never worked on Saturdays or any Jewish holidays when he was living in Hungary under the Communist regime. Somehow, this law was working for him and Ede was able to defend his position. Sorry to give the end away, but by now you already know Ede would succeed in whatever Ede wants to achieve.

After Ede came home from Budapest, he had to solve the last and final obstacle: get permission to work on Sunday instead of on Saturday. First, he visited his friend, Béla, who had been part of the Communist Leadership of Békéscsaba. Ede asked him to find the right person who would help along with this business enterprise. Béla was familiar with the local bureaucracy and promised to obtain all the necessary application forms to start the process. The next day, Jenő joined up with them to help complete all the paperwork. They spent a great deal of time to completing all the necessary applications for various permits and authorizations to open and operate a new factory. In addition, they submitted an operation plan for the factory that listed many important details that a government bureaucrat needed to know. It will employ 45 employees with various skills. For the production, the factory needs 9 sewing machines capable of producing leather goods and 28 metal stamps to cut the leather pieces, leather cutting knives and cutting boards, a typewriter and various other office and factory equipment. In addition, they drew up a plan to convert one of the underutilized buildings in the courtyard of the orthodox synagogue to serve as a factory building.

"This all looks good" Jenő said, "but I know without an official document from the State Department Store management, we will not be able succeed."

"So let us write one," Ede suggested, "when I was in Budapest I met Comrade Kiss, we could use his name. He is well connected."

"But without an official letterhead, signature, seals, and stamps this document will not be worth anything." Béla continued he truly knew all about the roadblocks of the current regime.

"No problem," Ede volunteered, "I will go back to Budapest, and I will get all the signatures and all the official stamps that we will need. I also have an official letterhead that we can use."

They then proceeded to create an official looking document that instructs Jenő and Ede to start the production as soon as possible. The document looked very good and it was ready to be signed. The three people were proud of the result.

In the following days, Ede collected all the signatures and official seals and paid all the dues requested in the various offices in Budapest. Among them was the most important one, the signature of Comrade Kiss along with his office's seal. Final letter:

STATE DEPARTMENT STORE
BUDAPEST HEADQUARTER
BUDAPEST
KOSSUTH LAJOS UTCA 6

Comrade Kiss the Chairman of the "Hungarian Socialist Workers Party" (Magyar Szocialista Munkás Párt) of the "State Department Store" headquartered in Budapest has decided that these proposed products (leather goods like belts, brief cases, ETC) are badly needed by the working people of Hungary.

The new factory must be located in Békéscsaba because the necessary skilled workers are ready to contribute to build the new socialist economy, are living in Békéscsaba. Mr. Jenő Katz will be the managing director responsible for the overall operation of the new factory including the responsibility of paying the employees.

Mr. Ede Kádár will manage the day-to-day operations, and will be responsible for all resource management that includes hiring workers and making sure that all the work is uninterrupted and products reach stores in a timely manner.

Unfortunately, the people having the skills required for the production are showing decadent religious tendencies and they are observing Saturday as their day of rest. Therefore, Comrade Kiss is ordering the six-day workweek to start on Sunday and end on Friday for this new factory, "Remnants and Waste Recovery Company" only.

Signed by

Dr. Gyula Kiss

Chairman, Hungarian Working People's Party

§ § § § § §

In the following few weeks, the construction work was completed, all equipment delivered, and in October 1949, the factory was in full operation. Out of the 45 workers, 36 were Jewish and nine were Seventh day Adventists.

Ede's hard work and determination created job opportunities for people who otherwise could not find any work to sustain decent lifestyle. The amount of money they were making was negligible, but during those trying years of the post-war era, living standards were very low. People did not need much to be happy. Everyone needed basic foodstuff, maybe an extra pair of shoes for a men or a pretty dress for a woman meant a great deal. Luxury was not in the dictionary of everyday people. Besides, only a few people could afford anything that would be considered luxury items. Even those who may be able to afford or some people who already had expensive things would be afraid to get them or display them. If a jealous neighbor, ambitious policeman, prying communist mole or simply their own child would say anything about their "extravagant" lifestyle, the secret police would show up at their doorstep and who knows what would happen next!

It was better to stay away from politics, live like most people live and be happy that one is alive, healthy and enjoy being with friends and family.

10

it is hard to be a
Jewish boy

Békéscsaba was a city located in the Great Plains (Alföld) and the
city was surrounded by some of the most fertile soil in Hungary. For
the most part, the city of Békéscsaba was a typical town of Hungary's
Great Plains. The agriculture provided most of the jobs for the residents and provided jobs for other industries associated with agriculture in and around Békéscsaba.

During the Turkish occupation of Hungary, Békéscsaba became
almost uninhabited; many were killed, others were enslaved and
taken to Turkey, and many simply ran away to find safe haven somewhere else. The Turkish occupiers were defeated by the Habsburgs in
the 17th century and by 1715, Békéscsaba was declared as a "ghost-
town." In 1718, János Harruckern, who earned distinction as a freedom fighter against the Turks, obtained Békés County and other
deserted areas in the neighboring counties as a gift from the
Habsburgs. Without people working in the fields, the fertile soil was
worthless. The new owner encouraged peasants from Slovak speaking territories in the north to move to Békéscsaba and to the surrounding areas. The Hungarian population called these people "tótok," a
Hungarian name for people of Slavic origin. Later in the 18th century,
Békéscsaba distinguished itself as the "Largest Village" of Europe. In
the middle of the 19th century, the arrival of the main railroad made
Békéscsaba an important transportation center that helped to develop
its commerce. By the middle if the twentieth century, the majority of
the population was mostly uneducated peasants and laborers. Jewish
merchants were attracted by the growing commerce of the area and
over the years, their numbers grew to over 3000 people. The Jewish

population brought their skills in commerce to the area. A small middle class also formed from the aristocracy, land and factory owners, and of course from the clergy.

Over the years of growth, the population reached over 50,000 people. Following the turbulent times after the war, the population shrunk to approximately 43,000 souls by 1949. The loss of most of the Jewish population and the Communist government's relocations of "undesirables" and other foreign nationals, mostly Germans, Slavs, and Romanians, caused the decline.

The concept of Anti-Semitism was not foreign to the local population of Békéscsaba. There were many who hated Jews. The similarity between anti-Semites and other racists was that they did not know the reason for their extreme dislike of the Jewish people and any other group of people who were the target of their hate. I guess these racists felt obligated to hate. They might want to prove to their contemporaries that they too wanted to support and continue the age-old hatred. On the other hand, the majority of Békéscsaba did not care one way or other. There was a small percentage of the population, mostly the better educated, who actually were looking for the friendship of the Jewish people.

The best way one could describe the social environment where Lacika was growing up. In the beginning, when he first became part of the Kádár family, none of this animosity affected his life. He was sheltered away from most outside influences. The neighbors knew that the Kádár family was Jewish, but most of them did not care. Some families were friendly with them. Their relationship with others would not go beyond saying "Good morning" or "Good bye."

§§§§§§

Kisvárda, a small town in the northern Great Plains was the birthplace of Ede. He lived in Kisvárda until he finished his schooling and obtained a high school diploma. His father was a "modern" orthodox Jew, who did not work on Saturday and Jewish holidays. Actually, the word "modern" was not used in association with orthodox Jews in those days. The family observed all Jewish dietary laws and all traditional customs and activities. Ede's father considered himself a Hungarian first, Jewish second, like many modern thinking educated Jews. He did have a beard but he and his family wore the same kind of attire that any well-dressed gentile would wear. His children, five girls and five boys, had a Jewish education, but they did not attend yeshivas (Jewish schools), they were attending public schools.

Because the family was observing Sabbath and all holidays, the children did not have to attend school during those days. The girls attended only the minimum schooling that the education laws required: sixth grade elementary school. The boys, on the other hand, attended gymnasiums (high schools in Hungary were called gimnázium.) Ede never mastered the Yiddish language; his parents did not speak Yiddish well either even though Ede's grandparents spoke fluent Yiddish. Since he studied German in school, he spoke German well, and he was able to follow Yiddish conversation and was able to make himself understood by the Yiddish speaking people.

If you are wondering about the history and the origin of the Yiddish language, let me give you a little history. The origin of the Yiddish language dates back to the 10th century Rhineland in Germany (the contemporary name is "Middle High German") used by the Ashkenazi Jews and mostly by Hassidic Jews today. The language spread mostly to Eastern European counties, like Poland, Russia, Ukraine, Lithuania, Romania, Galicia, ETC. In Hungary, mostly the very religious Jews spoke Yiddish and those who immigrated to Hungary from Poland or Russia.

§ § § § § §

Nagydobos, a tiny village about 35 kilometers southeast of Kisvárda was the birthplace of Helen. The small Jewish population of the town never exceeded more than 15 to 20 families. Helen's grandfather moved to Nagydobos from Poland, following many fellow Polish Jews seeking more freedom in Hungary after the Austro-Hungarian Compromise of 1867 established the Dual Monarchy of Austria-Hungary. The constitution of the Dual Monarchy established equal-rights for the Jewish population with their Christian neighbors. In Nagydobos, Jews and non-Jews maintained a peaceful coexistent. Her father owned a "Country Store," where almost everything that the locals needed could be bought with the exception of foodstuff. Her six brothers attended Yeshivas (Jewish religious schools) and they studied until they learned enough to be able to obtain a "semicha lerabbanut" (Rabbinical ordination). However, none of them became practicing Rabbis. The three girls received traditional religious studies, which prepared them to become good housewives and mothers. Everyone in her family fully conversed in "Mame-Loshin" (the mother tongue) that was most commonly known as Yiddish.

§ § § § § §

We need to understand how a three years old child may feel in a strange house with strange customs. On one hand, Ede and Helen gave him loving tender care, the kind of care that Lacika in his short life had never experienced. On the other hand, Lacika had to learn many rules that were dictated by the fact that the Kádár family followed orthodox Jewish laws. These rules, at times, burdened Lacika so much that he wished to run away. This reminds me of the time when Lacika, who was about five years old, bravely stood in front of his mother and declared:

"I am running away!" Helen was smiling and decided to go along with his decision and asked him:

"Where are you going?"

"I do not know, but I do not like it here anymore." What triggered his determination of running away? Lacika wanted to play, but he had not completed his obligatory chores. A chore like saying a required prayer of the day or washing his hand before the meal, who remembers, and Helen stopped him and Lacika got angry.

"I know you may need some clothes and some food on your journey, don't you?" Helen had a hard time holding back her laugh when she was looking at his serous face.

"I think… I could use some food or some cookies," he mumbled. He was not so sure, what would happen next.

"Do you remember some fairy tales I was reading to you? Just like in these fables, I will make a backpack for you." Helen got a large kerchief, folded it into a triangle, and put some cookies on top of it. She folded it again so the cookies would not fall out. Finally, she tied the kerchief on one end of a stick, just like in the fairytales the hobo's drum looked like, and gave it to Lacika. Lacika was surprised about his mother's coolness, but like a "man," he put the package on his shoulder and bravely headed out to the street. Of course, Helen was watching him, but did not interfere. Lacika started to walk toward the main street. When he got there, he stopped because he could not make up his mind to go left, right or cross the street and go straight. While he was standing there, he told himself:

"I must go to the railroad station. Walking would not take me far enough. I need to take a train to travel far." Therefore, he turned right.

"I have no money, how could I get on the train?" Nevertheless, this minor detail did not stop him on his journey, but slowed him down thinking where should he go. In the meantime, Ede had come home.

"What are you watching?" he asked Helen.

"Do you see Lacika across the park; he is 'running away!'" Helen answered with a big smile on her face.

"He does not seem to run, he is walking rather slowly."

"I guess he ran out of steam. See, now he is turning into the park, going across and heading home. I knew this would happen." Helen was amused about this run-away adventure. Lacika came into the house and sat down by the kitchen table. He opened up his hobo's drum and started to eat the cookies.

"Did you get hungry during your 'world tour'?" Ede was asking his son.

"Yea."

"How come you are back to home so soon?"

"I got tired."

"But you are supposed to be running away. How come you are here?" Ede was teasing him.

"I changed my mind that is all," Lacika answered with a little bit of annoyance in his voice and got up, indicating the "conversation is over" and went into his room. Ede and Helen, ever since, teased Lacika about this "incident." In addition, this funny event provided a source for delightful moments when Helen and Ede enlightened their friends with the story of "when Lacika ran away." The reality was that running away would never be a correct decision for his problems; but I am going too fast.

§ § § § § §

Let me slow down and describe a typical day for Lacika when he was about five or six years old. The first thing after getting up in the morning, Lacika had to wash his hands and face in cold water, which was not necessarily a bad thing. Unlike today, most families did not have hot water ready at all times. In the summer, the refreshing cold water was a blessing. Speaking of which, after the wash, Lacika had to recite the Modeh Ani (אֲנִי מוֹדֶה—Blessing after Arising) prayer, which was traditionally recited by all religious Jews to thank G-d for returning their soul, so they could serve G-d for another day. Krijat Shema al-Hamitah must be said before one goes to sleep; Lacika had to say this prayer loud no matter how sleepy he was.

Washing hands before a meal was also a very good idea, but saying a prayer or blessing (Brachot) after it may not be the most enjoyable task for a five years old child. Do not stop now! It continues. Before eating anything, there were different blessings for most food types: one blessing for fruits from trees, one blessing for vegetables, one blessing for bread, one blessing for cookies, one blessing for drinks, yet another blessing for wine or grape juice. There were prayers for the beginning of a meal and there were prayers after you finish your meal. Did you get it? Yes? Take a deep breath, more rules to come: There was a blessing when you wore something new or ate something for the first time this year, there was a blessing for seeing a rainbow, and there was a blessing when you hear thunder. Is it enough? I think it is, but I did not even come close to finishing the list. Do not worry. I will not continue listing them all; I do not want you to fall asleep.

Of course, Lacika had no idea for the reasons to say all these payers and blessings or had any idea as to the significance of these prayers. He did not speak Hebrew or Yiddish, and his father most of the time did not bother to explain the rationale for all these customs.

People, who are not familiar with Jewish customs, may find it unusual that Lacika had to learn to read Hebrew before he learned to read and write in Hungarian, his native language. This phenomenon was not an unusual or unheard of trend within the Orthodox Jewish community at all. Indeed, Lacika at the age of five was already behind the "normal" schedule for the customary Jewish education. He was late because Ede felt that Lacika should not start his Jewish studies until he got more comfortable in the Kádár family and he felt more at ease in his new environment.

Lacika's education started with learning the Hebrew alphabet (aleph-bet). Ede took up the task of teaching him. You must know that Hebrew letters are hard to learn because some letters may be represented in two different forms depending on what position in the word these letters are used. For instance, the letter "Mem" looks like this מ, when used in the middle of the word, but if "Mem" used at the end of a word, it would look like this ם, not to be confused with the letter "Somech," which looks like this ס. In addition, each of the 22 letters of the Hebrew alphabet is considered a consonant. A system of dots helps to determine the vowels. I do not want to bore you with many more examples of how confusing reading Hebrew text is, especially if one does not understand what is being read. It is complicated, but with practice, anything could be learned. For a long time Lacika constantly confused letters: "Hei" ה, "Vov" ו, "Zayin" ז. Why? Who knows? It took a lot of patience from Ede to teach Lacika how to read the Hebrew text. Now Lacika was ready to pray properly in the Synagogue and at home. He did not enjoy reading Hebrew, but he was kind of proud of his achievement and many times, he even pretended to pray with enthusiasm.

His way of life was definitely changed. Among the changes were the Friday evening "nightmares." Every Friday night after Ede and Lacika came home from the Synagogue services, Lacika had to recite the prayer "Shalom Aleichem" and the following prayer "Ashes Chayil." Without fail, almost every Friday night the following inter-actions or some variation thereof, between Ede and Lacika took place:

"Shalom Aleichem, Aleichem Shalom," Lacika started to read, long pause followed, "I do not want to say it," he said swallowing his tears. He was very hungry. He was sleepy. It was late at night and his normal bedtime had already passed. Besides, he hated this responsi-bility but was afraid to complain to his father. Lacika was trying to do anything to find an excuse not to say these prayers.

"You must read it," Ede answered forcefully and pointed to the prayer book to continue. Helen was quietly sitting by the dining table watching the interaction, but she never said much. She never inter-fered, as if she agreed with these "punishments." Lacika continued to read, but a few words later stopped again.

"I cannot continue," Lacika told his father, crying, but still with some dignity in his voice.

"I do not want to hear you crying. You know very well by now, Lacika that we will not start dinner until you have finished the read-ing."

"I do not care about the food! I want to go to sleep!" Lacika answered with a full-blown crying voice and with a bit more determi-nation. He knew better, he has a losing case, but he tried this almost every single Friday night (maybe not every Friday night, but often enough). This time Ede just stared at him without saying a word. Lacika continued to read, but stopped again after reading a few more words.

"I am telling you; I cannot read anymore, I have a headache."

"I am sorry about your headache, but you know very well, you must finish it! This is your responsibility as a Jewish boy"

"Mommy, may I go to sleep now, I will finish it tomorrow, prom-ise" directing his request to Helen, hoping for some support from his beloved mother. Disappointingly, she still did not say a word.

"But Mommyeee!" he screamed with a high-pitched voice and his face was soaked with his pouring tears.

"Please Lacika, listen to your Dad, you must finish the prayer as a good Jewish boy should," came a polite request from Helen. In the past, she had a few words with Ede about these Friday nights, but Ede was stubborn as a mule and he would not allow under any circumstances to change the Friday night practice. He strongly believed that his child must learn that it is not so easy to be a Jewish boy, and he guaranteed that he would not make it any easier for his son.

§ § § § § §

Jewish religious law prohibits cooking on the Sabbath. Firewood and coal was used in most ovens in Hungary in those days. During the winter, one of the favorite foods of Jews was cholent, a traditional Jewish stew simmered overnight and eaten for lunch on Sabbaths. First, the cholent was cooked before sundown on Friday and put into an oven. Since religious Jews could not keep up the fire on Shabbat, people took the pot to the local bakery (non-Jewish) for overnight baking. Coming home from shul, Lacika had to carry the pot home since before his bar mitzvah, a Jewish child did not have to obey all the laws of Judaism.

Attending the regular services in the Synagogue was mandatory for Lacika. Even on the rare occasions that they did not go to the Synagogue services, Lacika had to say all the required prayers at home or wherever they were at the time, when prayers were in order. Jews are required to pray three times a day: morning, afternoon and night.

Jewish boys celebrate their Bar Mitzvah, this expression literary means "son of the commandment" on their 13th birthday and according to Jewish laws, a boy becomes a man. As a man, from that day forward the young boy would be accountable for all his actions in front of G-d. Before Lacika's Bar Mitzvah, he was allowed to say a shortened version of the Morning Prayer. It was mandatory to recite a blessing before and after every meal and say all other blessings required for many different occasions. After his Bar Mitzvah, Lacika must conclude his morning prayers before he could go to school or do anything else in the morning. Sometimes, he got away without saying the required evening prayers. Again, I am going too fast.

§ § § § § §

In the 1949, 1950 timeframe, Békéscsaba still had an active Jewish community. Since school-age children had to attend public schools, the Jewish community had the traditional after-school program (Héder) set up for the Jewish education of the children of the community. The method of teaching used was based upon the assumption that when children repeat the information presented to them often enough, the child will remember it forever. The teacher would read a few words from the Torah in Hebrew then translate these words into Yiddish. The boys (girls did not attended Héder) would repeat whatever the teacher was saying until everyone memorized the text. Ede believed memorization was the best way to learn, but did not like the teaching method used in the Héder. Ede was convinced that since Lacika did not speak or understand Yiddish, he would not learn anything useful attending the Héder.

The big synagogue was not used for the everyday prayer services. During winter, it was difficult and too expensive to heat the big synagogue. The smaller Bais Hamidrash (house of learning) was used for Sabbath services in the winter and it was used for daily services too.

About a half a block down the side street of the large synagogue, there was a building owned by the Jewish community. From the street, it looked like a typical one-story city house. A large gate opened into a courtyard surrounded by several interconnected buildings. The first door after entering into the courtyard was the apartment of the Shamash, the community's caretaker, everybody's Uncle Yayli. The second door was the men's entry into the Beit Hamidrash, the next door was used by the women. The prayer room doubled as an all-purpose activity/school building. A long table near the entrance door served as a place where classes for Héder were kept and for Shaleshides (the Hungarian pronunciation of Shalosh Seudot,) the customary gathering after Sabbath services. Further down in the courtyard, a door led to a passageway to the next courtyard. These passageways connecting joining courtyards were used by many Jewish communities, because religious Jews cannot carry anything outside of their own courtyard on Sabbath. This solution would give an opportunity to "bypass" the rule of carrying within the community center.

In this courtyard was the apartment of Mr. Neiman, the religious teacher, the shochet of the community. In addition, the ritual bathhouse was also located in this courtyard. Lacika went to these baths many times with his father. People, who never had the "pleasure" of visiting this kind of ritual bath, would think this place looked especially strange. Men and women would visit in different times, not only because of religious reasons. One should not immerse in this common pool of water having any garments on. In other words, everyone was buck-naked with the exception of a tiny apron covering (somewhat) the "private parts." I do not have to tell you that this place was not one of the favorite places of Lacika. He did not mind using the available private hot water tub used for bathing with his father, but the big pools…forget it.

Lacika quite frequently visited the buildings of the Jewish community. He saw the Héder in action. An older bocher (Jewish Student) normally was "teaching" the younger kids. They all kept repeating everything that the older boy was saying. After awhile, he would stop, and ask one of the kids to recite what they were learning before. When the kid would make a mistake, the older kid would scream at the poor boy, and if more mistakes were made, he would punish the student. His favorite punishment was asking the "guilty one" to place his hand on the table and the overzealous "teacher" would use the edge of a large hardcover book to strike his hand. If it sounds horrible, it was. Can you imagine how much pain a heavy book and a sadistic kid could cause? Seeing this, Lacika was so happy that his father did not make him go to the Héder. Corporal punishment was more or less an accepted practice in the education system and at home.

When Lacika was about seven years old, Ede hired an old retired teacher, Mr. Kleinman. Mr. Kleinman was living in a Jewish old age home in Békéscsaba, which was one of the few remaining Jewish homes in Hungary. Mr. Kleinman was a Hebrew teacher before he retired; he was familiar with the Jewish religious teachings, but he had never been a religious person himself. He was teaching elementary school so he knew very well how to catch small children's attention. He was a wonderful teacher with lot patience. Ede explained to him the circumstances with Lacika and he decided that the best way to teach Lacika was to tell him stories about the religion and Jewish history.

Lacika became interested in religion while Mr. Kleinman was teaching him. To illustrate the reason for this interest, let me tell you some of the stories told by Mr. Kleinman.

The prayer "Aleinu" (עָלֵינוּ)—a prayer that being recited three times a day after the three daily prayers. "Aleinu" went in front of G-d and complained to G-d that G-d is so unfair. Why should "Aleinu" always be the last prayer to be said, it means that he is not considered an important prayer like many other prayers. G-d promised to rectify the situation and G-d awarded "Aleinu" by making him an important part of the set of prayers that would be said only on Yom Kippur, the holiest holiday of the Jewish people. From this point on "Aleinu" was very proud of himself.

This little memorable story, a fable, stayed with Lacika all his life that taught him several things about Jewish prayers (weekday, high holidays, etc) and gave him encouragement to stand up for his rights.

Let me tell another story also about Yom Kippur, the holiest day for Jews.

Yom Kippur was approaching fast. A poor man was walking home, but he was not able to walk fast enough to get home before sundown. As a religious Jew, he could not continue his journey home. What could he do? He stopped to spend the night and the following day in a strange place and he did not even have anything to eat for dinner. He also had another problem, he wanted to pray to god, but he could not because he did not know the Yom Kippur prayers by heart. He was thinking hard, but he could not remember any of the prayers. Finally, he started to recite the aleph-bet and he was saying it until the holy day was over.

In the meantime, a rich man spent his Yom Kippur services in his beautiful synagogue and said all the prayers that needed to be said. G-d received all prayers and he liked the prayer of the poor man better than he liked the rich man's prayer. The rich man went to complain to G-d.

"How could you do this to me? He did not even say a single prayer, I was praying to you all day; I said all the prayers that were required."

"I know that," G-d replied. "It was not what you said; it was how you said it that was important to me. The poor man put all his heart into his payer even when he did not know the words. You were saying all the words, but your heart was not in them."

§ § § § §

Lacika was looking forward to these and many other wonderful stories told by Mr. Kleinman. These stories made Lacika curious about the Jewish religion. Later, when Lacika learned to read and write in Hungarian, Ede gave him the Hungarian translation of the five books of the Torah and other books that are considered part of the Jewish Bible, also known as the Old Testament. On long Saturdays, when Lacika's activities were limited, he was reading these books with a great deal of interest. All this interest was triggered by the enthusiastic teachings of Mr. Kleinman. Lacika was looking forward to seeing this kind old man and listening to his stories and his explanation of ancient Jewish history. Yes, the teachings of Mr. Kleinman were more like fairy-tales, a little bit of history and very little religion. At home, Lacika's father taught him that being a Jew was the same as being religious. Obeying all the rules of religion and being a Jew, the two cannot be separated from each other. From Mr. Kleinman Lacika learned that being a Jew was much more than religion. There was a whole world out there for Jews to learn that has nothing to do with religion; it had a lot to do with Jewish traditions and pride.

Mr. Kleinman taught Lacika for several years before he died. Lacika was about 12 years old when he was left without a Jewish teacher. He missed the old man. He did not miss the religious aspect of the classes, but he enjoyed the way Mr. Kleinman was teaching him. Lacika was approaching his Bar Mitzvah age and Ede needed to find someone for the Bar Mitzvah preparation, Ede had to find another Jewish educator.

Ede visited the old-age home frequently to support and care for these old people, who were mostly left without any relatives. He convinced Mr. Haas, also a retired teacher, to work with Lacika. After his salary was negotiated, Ede hired him to teach Lacika every weekday for one hour. In truth, he did not measure up to Mr. Keinman's standards. I am not sure Ede ever questioned the teaching skills of Mr. Haas. Ede was busy making a life and for some reason he trusted Mr. Haas. Lacika did not like his new teacher at all. Ede would not listen to any complaints about attending the Jewish studies, so Lacika tried to make the best of this situation. The old age home was about a kilometer away, Mr. Haas was not young and he had a hard time walking to Ede's house. Since Lacika was already a "big boy," he rode his bicycle to his lessons that normally lasted for an hour, more or less, mostly less.

Studies with his new teacher were not successful. Lacika found the teaching boring and a waste of time. Lacika did not like the man and did not like the way he was teaching. Truthfully, Lacika hardly learned anything during the year or so when he was going to see Mr. Haas. Many times, he did not show up for these boring lessons but rather took his bicycle to ride around the town to explore the city. Mr. Haas' lessons were not organized. Mr. Haas mostly discussed the weekly readings from the Torah and provided some limited simplistic translations of the Torah's text. The difference between studying in the Héder and studying with Mr. Haas was that Mr. Haas was willing to translate the Torah to Hungarian instead of Yiddish. Most of the explanations provided by Mr. Haas did not make much sense to Lacika. Additional questions were "tolerated" but not welcomed. Mr. Haas rarely provided any interesting answers to his questions. Many questions were dismissed by saying "some questions Jews should not ask, because we should not question G-d's will." Lacika believed that this man probably just did not know the answers. He was missing the wonderful stories that had been told by Mr. Kleinman. The old man did not really care about teaching anything to Lacika. Mr. Haas never said anything to Ede about the missed lessons, because he was afraid that Ede would fire him and his extra income would disappear.

After Lacika was called upon the Torah for his Bar Mitzvah and read the Haphtarah portion, the whole synagogue was impressed. The Haphtarah is a short selection from the Prophets read on every Sabbath following the reading from the Torah.

Most Jews in Békéscsaba took advantage of the volatile situation following the Hungarian Revolution against the domination of the Soviet Union in November of 1956, and immigrated to the west. Only a handful Jews remained in Békéscsaba. Older Jews stayed because they were afraid to cross the border by foot to avoid the border guards. Some others, for one reason or other, could not or were afraid to leave their home again.

Ede stayed because he and Helen were afraid to make the long trip to the Austrian border, which was over 400 kilometers away. They were not sure that Helen would be able to make the trip due her poor health.

After 1956, the majority of the religious kids were left with their parents. Most Jews who continued to live in Békéscsaba did not attend Synagogue services with any regularity; their children were almost completely separated from Jewish life. Lacika was the only religious child. Rabbi Schnitzler and his family left for England and Lacika was one of the very few kids who could read the Hebrew prayer books. The new Rabbi had a son who was much younger than Lacika and was probably the only other kid who could read and regularly attended the synagogue. Hearing a child reciting the Haphtarah under these circumstances was impressive. Ede's insistence on a Jewish education of Lacika was working out for the better; at least this was the opinion of Ede.

11

working parents

The Remnants and Waste Recovery Company was established and it was open for business. Before any production could be started, Ede had to find the way to train his so-called "skilled" workers. Most of his employees did not have the slightest idea how to produce leather goods. For many of them, this was the first menial job they ever had. Before the war, many of them were housewives, intellectuals, business owners, and educators, the kind of people who were not welcomed in the communist world. They had no idea how to use a hammer or what a sewing machine looks like (a little bit of exaggeration on my part.) They came to make some money to improve their lives during these hard times. Some were there because the communists would not trust them in their own professions, these people belonged to the "non-desired" class of people, and they were labeled as "enemies of the state."

One of the workers was Helen. For the first time in many years, she was working using her sewing skills. She was one of nine who were assigned to stitch together the triangular pieces for the briefcases. Under the harsh economic times, it became necessary for women to work outside the home to earn some additional money for their family. Helen did not mind working, but she missed Lacika. Helen's skills were important for the new factory since she was one of the few who knew how to use the sewing machine and she was able to teach others.

It took several weeks until the "production" became a smooth operation. Each phase of each product was completed by different people. The production operated almost like an assembly line. Some were stamping the leather pieces, some were pasting them on paper, and some were sewing the pieces to the cloth backing. Two workers were cutting the constructed pieces into the desired sizes and finally some were sewing together the individual pieces to create the brief-case. Ede took care of most of the factory administration and took care of all personnel issues. He also made sure that all manufacturing materials were on hand by the time workers needed them.

§ § § § § §

In the beginning of Helen's renewed working career, she was worried about Lacika. What would happen to him while she was working? There was a kindergarten a couple of blocks away from the house. Helen enrolled Lacika to try it. Helen was hoping it would work out and Lacika would be under adult supervision during the day while she was working. Kindergartens were not mandatory in the 1950s.

The education system did not believe in teaching under-school-age children to read and write or to get familiar with numbers. The good thing about kindergarten was that children were under supervision with various activities to keep them occupied. Working parents could breathe easier knowing their children were in good hands. Activities were not educational in the traditional sense. Kindergarten teachers were teaching kids to sing some newly created or slightly modified children's songs with "hidden" messages about the great life under communism. One of these songs was based upon an old Hungarian children play-song like this:

Children form a circle and one kid would stand in the middle. The kids start to sing:

"In the middle there is a girl"

"In the middle a little girl is waiting"

"Let us see whom she chooses"

"Let us see who she loves the best"

"Let us join in when they dance"

The kid in the middle chooses someone from the circle; they hold hands and swirls around while they sing the following:

"With iron and fire we will protect the peace"

"We will fight for a world without fright"

"To have peace for all our might"

Even to you the reader, this little play-song might not sounded unusual; you must step back and think. Then, you may come to the realization that they were teaching four and five years olds to use iron and fire (meaning weapons) against the frightening world (people who were against the communists), against people whose identities were unknown to these little kids. Do not worry, in a few years when these children go to school, they would be told many times over who these "unspeakable" people we, the good Communist, must fight against. The pre-conditioning was started at early age. Just like it was done in Nazi Germany.

§ § § § § §

After the first day that Lacika came back from the kindergarten, Helen asked him,

"So, how was your day?"

"Okay," he answered.

"Did you like it?"

"No."

"Why not?"

"I do not know."

"Did other kids bother you? Was the teacher rude? What was wrong there?"

"I did not like how the place smelled, I do not want to go there again!" Helen did not force the issue and did not ask any more questions. Lacika's kindergarten days were over, even before it started.

During winter, Lacika would start his typical day eating a hearty breakfast. He liked to sleep late, still does even today. On most days, Helen prepared Lacika's breakfast before she left for work. After he woke up, he gobbled down his food and played in the comfort of the warm family bedroom, where all of them slept. Ede always made sure that the fire was lit in the fireplace before he left for work. The beautiful fireplace would keep the room warm for most of the day. He played with the few toys he had, kids did not have as many toys as kids would have today. He listened to music and other programs on the two available stations on the radio.

Let us stop for a moment; I know what you are thinking. "How could parents leave a four or five year old child alone in a house?" You are right to think this way, but… Times were different then.

§ § § § § §

In the early 1950s, life was simple and relatively peaceful for most people. Aside from the political turmoil, aside from having financial issues, most people lived their lives to the fullest possible. People in those days had different attitudes toward each other. Unlike today, people were willing to help each other as much as they could; this phenomenon was not unique to the Hungarian people, many other parts of the world people behaved similarly. In any particular neighborhood, even in larger cities, most people knew each other. Some knew each other only by crossing their way on the streets, but in need, they would help each other. People spent their free time socializing. It seems that in those days people did have more time for friends compared to today's fast-moving, always-busy times. There were no phones to call ahead before one would go to visit a friend. People would show up at their friend's doorsteps without any warning or "appointment." If the friend were not home, not a problem, the visitor would come back some other time with no hard feelings. If people were at home, the visitors were welcomed at anytime, invited or otherwise. Friends always were offered something to drink, coffee or tea and something to eat like cookies or other snacks.

Televisions were not yet available to "entertain"; only one or two stations were available on the radio. The library was open for everyone with books for every taste. One always found something that helped to kill time. Even kids have never complained about boredom. People in general would read more books than we do today. Record players were also a good source of entertainment, occasional movies or a play in the local theaters completed most people's entertainment needs.

Crime was virtually unheard of. Most people did not even bother to lock their doors, only if they left town, maybe... After all, Hungary was a police state. Crime was harshly punished and overall security was very good. Neighbors would look after their neighbors. Neighbors were looking after each other's property, children, and anything else valuable. When Helen and Ede were at work, they were confident that the five-year-old Lacika would be safe at home. Besides, their work place was only a ten-minute walk from their house. Roaming the streets in Békéscsaba in those days was also relatively safe. With the exception of some horse-drawn wagons and some public transportation buses, the streets were clear from traffic. Owning an automobile was not possible for the majority of the population. Automobiles were usually only owned by some larger corporations and government agencies. Most people used their bicycles to go anywhere within the city. For longer trips, people were taking buses or trains. Even policemen were walking or sometimes using their bicycles to get to places. At most, there were a couple of police cars in the entire city of over 50,000 inhabitants. Automobiles were expensive to keep even for the government.

§ § § § § §

When Lacika got bored during the day, he could walk over to some of his friend's houses to play. One of his neighbors was the Rattai family. The husband was working as a radio and other small electronics repairman and he was hardly home. The wife was taking care of their home and children. She did not have a job outside the home. They had two children, one girl, Baba, who was about the same age as Lacika and a boy, Jancsi, who was a couple years younger. Lacika liked this girl. They were playing together anytime they had the chance and they kept their friendship for many years to come.

The house where the Rattai family was living represented a somewhat typical house in Békéscsaba. The long building extended deep into the courtyard. Only one room of the whole house faced the street. A long wooden fence was erected between the house and neighboring properties, just like most houses in the neighborhood. The fence that was facing the street had one entry for people and a gate for carriages. Along the long walkway leading to their residence was a large vegetable garden, which belonged to another family living in the front part of the house. Lacika had never known these people, since they kept to themselves. The Rattai family occupied the rear end of the long house. A pigpen was located behind the house where there was always several stinking pigs kept. Many people raised pigs in their backyard. Since pigs would eat practically anything, it was an economical way to "reuse" (recycle) household waste. People would kill these animals in the fall season. The pig provided ham, bacon, lard and the famous Hungarian sausages and kielbasa. Lacika on the other hand, regretfully so, never tasted any of these "goodies" since they were not kosher. Beyond the pigpen, the family also had a vegetable garden with a few fruit trees behind the building. Aunt Rattai was supplementing her income by helping Helen. For many years, she was helping Helen with some of her housework like cleaning the house, laundry, canning fruits and vegetables and in the winter months lighting the fire in the tile stove on Saturdays.

The other family that Lacika was visiting was the Kovács family. They had two boys, a seven years old Sanyi, and a nine years old Misi. Both boys were a little bit older than Lacika, but the three were playing together very well. Their mother did not work, so when Lacika would come over, he was well taken care of with cookies, cakes, and other goodies for snacks. They understood and respected that the Kádár family was Jewish and their son would not eat non-kosher food with the exception of dairy products. Kovács family's apartment occupied part of a larger house on the corner of the same street where Lacika's house was. Their windows were facing the main avenue that stretches between the railroad station and the main square of the downtown business area of Békéscsaba. The apartment house was a single story corner house and two other families occupied the rest of the building. Their backyard, unlike the backyard of the Rattai family, looked more like a residential city courtyard. Large trees and flowerbeds were occupying the open spaces of the yard instead of a vegetable garden. Lacika never knew what kind of job the father had, but the family lived well, they had nice furniture and the kids wore nice clothing.

Ever since Helen started working, she had to cook after she came home from work and on Fridays. On Fridays, she did not go work to give her time to prepare the food for Saturday. As an orthodox Jew, she would not prepare any food on Sabbaths. For lunch, Helen and Ede went home and this way the family could eat together. It was hard for Helen, but they did not have any other choices for financial reasons.

§ § § § § §

The upkeep of a kosher house was hard and more expensive than keeping a non-kosher household. Most housewives, especially Jewish ones, had to work hard to prepare food for their family. Ready-made foods were limited and kosher ones were unheard of. Housewives had to go to the open market to buy fresh vegetables and fruits. They also bought chickens, ducks, or gooses. To make it kosher, they went to the religious slaughterhouse, and then they had to clean off all the feathers by hand which was just the beginning of the "process." Meat products must go through several steps to make them kosher. After the animal was killed, their blood must be completely drained. Jews are not allowed to eat blood. The meat must be soaked in water for an hour, followed by salting the meat generously all over. A half hour later, the excess salt must be washed off. Now, it was ready to cook. Gas ranges were not available for most people in the 1950s. To cook, we need heat; to make heat, wood and coal was needed. Someone had to bring the wood and coal to the house after the wood was chopped into small pieces to start up the fire in the stove. After all this, the housewife could start the cooking. Most husbands were at work and they were expecting fresh, hot meals for lunch or dinner. You get the idea. Family mealtime was cherished by everyone and mealtimes were strictly enforced by parents.

The winter was finally over. The nice warm spring air encourages people and nature alike to refresh, to come alive again from the hibernation of winter. The bright sunshine broke the winter depression and brought smiles to people's faces. Lacika finally could easily roam around the neighborhood, without worrying about catching a cold. He had a lot of free time most of the day, his parents been working so he was alone in the house. He spent his time with his new friends in the neighborhood. Now he could play soccer or other ballgames with his friends, getting into the normal mischief's that boy's normally would get into.

Spring was over and the summer heat arrived. South Hungary could have very hot summers. During the summer months, there was hardly any rain to provide relief from the dry heat. The streets were covered with dried dust from the sandy earth of Békéscsaba. Occasionally, a light wind would pick up the hot sand and mix it with the hot air. Sometimes these mixtures would end up on your face, in your eyes. There was no relief from the heat until the fall. Summer time was not necessary the best season in these parts of Hungary. A child like Lacika, growing up in this environment, may not notice any of these inconveniences; these would become part of everyday life. Lacika was a child who wants to do something that kills his boredom. He did not know how to read yet, he will start school in the fall, he was always looking for something new, something interesting to do.

§ § § § § §

The factory for the Remnants and Waste Recovery Company was set up in the courtyard of the Orthodox synagogue. The courtyard was partitioned into two halves. The two yards were separated by a long fence with a gate to allow movement between the two sections. On one side was the impressive looking building of the synagogue with a well-kept garden. The worshippers used the entrance from a busy main street. On the other side of the property, there were several buildings and a separate entrance from the side street. The caretaker had an apartment in one of the buildings. He was responsible for maintaining the grounds and the synagogue. He also took care of the maintenance of all other buildings in the complex. The caretaker had two daughters. The older one was a 16 years old teenager, causing a great deal of headaches for her parents. She was in constant trouble with her boyfriends, school, and numerous other issues. The younger girl was about eight or nine years old, a typical "Tom-boy." She also had her share of trouble making; the good news was she had no boyfriend yet. A large building was converted to the factory for Remnants and Waste Recovery Company. This building originally was used to store various equipment and supplies. Some of these were moved into the basement of the Synagogue and stored in the attics of other buildings.

Two other structures were also standing on the property. One of them was the ritual slaughterhouse, where the shochet (ritual slaughterer) were slaughtering chickens, gooses, ducks, and other feathered animals in a manner that they could become consumable for the people who prefer consuming kosher meat. This building always smelled from the blood of the slaughtered animals and flocks of flies always greeted the people who came by. Lacika did not like to go near to this place.

The last building on the complex did not smell very well either. It was a large outhouse. One side for the men's urinals and stalls, the other side for women and obviously with stalls only. Especially in the summer months, hundreds of flies provided entertainment and annoyance at the same time, by buzzing around enjoying their source of food in both of these buildings.

You the reader have to forgive me. I am describing real life in the 1950s, the way it was, no whitewashing. Outhouses like this were part of the everyday life of that era, especially in the countryside. Most houses in rural areas did not have any indoor plumbing and people had to go somewhere! Can you imagine a cold, freezing winter and you have to go? Do not think about it! The reason I am describing this building is to set the stage for an unusual experience for Lacika that played out there. You may not found it so unusual. Maybe? Please! Do not think about anything bad. You have to wait until we get there.

§ § § § § §

Sometimes, Lacika went to see his parents at their place of work. While he was hanging around in the courtyard, he met a girl who was a little bit older than he was. They started to talk and as children many times do, they became friends. Who was this girl? Well, she was the daughter of the caretaker of the synagogue. Her name was Kati. It is not important for the story who was she, but what she has done or made Lacika do. This was the reason she became part of this story.

The two, Lacika and Kati, became good friends. Most afternoons, they were hanging around and playing games, all sorts of games. Since she was a "Tom-boy," the two have challenged each other into various activities, the kind of activities that most girls usually would not get into. Some of these challenges were somewhat dangerous and some of them were outright silly. Lacika enjoyed this, since he never met a girl like her. Baba, the neighbor's daughter, was wild, but nothing like this one.

One day, the two were playing some silly games as usual; Lacika had to go to pee. He ran into the men's urinal section of the outhouse and started to do what he needed to do. He looks up, Kati was standing over him, and she was staring at his...

"What are you doing? he shyly asked the girl.

"Nothing, I am just looking at it!"

"What are you looking at?

"Nothing," she said with a smile. "Do you want to see mine?" Without waiting for Lacika's answer, she lifted up her skirt and revealed what was underneath. Lacika's eyes popped open, he never seen anything like this. Then, he bent down to have a closer look and with a very convinced voice, he concluded:

"Something is missing there."

"You silly child, nothing is missing. This is why we are girls and not boys."

"But, how do you...?"

"You don't know anything," she angrily replied. "We sit down to pee. This how girls do it. What a baby you are!"

Lacika face lit up after he understood the explanation. Aha, now he has something over her. Lacika never won any challenges between the two of them. Finally, he has the G-d given winning advantage over this girl, and quickly made the challenge with a certain confidence in his voice:

"I bet you that you cannot pee standing up!" He had a big smile on his face, but not for long. Kati went over the urinal and Lacika could not believe his eye, she was doing it. True, it went all over, but she beat him again. Lacika had enough; he tried to make a dignified exit from the outhouse, and did not stop until he got home. He did not go back to the synagogue courtyard for days. After all, he had to have his self-respect!

Well, if a "man" has a "girlfriend," how can he stay away? Truth was Lacika could not stay away. Finally, he swallowed his pride and he went to see Kati again. After all, he had time, did not have to do anything important, he was in the neighborhood anyway, why not.

"Hello," he said when he noticed Kati playing outside of her house.

"Hello," she replied, not even looking at him. She was busy doing something, which at this time seemed important; she was ignoring him, maybe?

"What are you doing?"

"Nothing"

"Do you want to do something?"

"Not really." However, at this time, Kati looked at him from the corner of her eye. She was watching his reaction to the answers. It was all pretend.

"Okay," replied Lacika, with a disappointed tone in his voice. His "love" was so indifferent! What is going on? He did not understand this. "Well," he told himself, "this is life, and life is full of disappointments." He did not yet understand how "women's" minds were working. He hardly reached the street, when he heard Kati's voice.

"Do you want to go to the riverbank?"

"Yes!" He answered with enthusiasm and ran back to her. You fool; you do not know how you have been played. I guess he had to start learning the complicated interactions between the sexes.

The two walked through the downtown area to the banks of the Kőrös River. The downtown area was a wide park-like street, with rows of large trees along the sidewalks on both sides of the roadway. There was an additional pedestrian walkway sandwiched between the lines of trees. Numerous park benches provided a place to sit down and escape the strong rays of the sun or to watch other people shopping, walking, or taking care of some personal business.

Everyone in Békéscsaba called it a "river," but it was in fact a dead-end branch of the real Kőrös River, its water level was controlled by a water gate. Nevertheless, the riverbank was very nice. Branches of large willow trees were almost touching the water, creating a romantic spot for the local lovebirds. Old trees of all kinds lined up on both sides of riverbank. Walkways paralleling the waterway and benches were placed on various locations to offer peaceful resting areas to the public. Several bridges connected the main city area with the garden like residential area of Békéscsaba. This area was always frequented by people looking to relax during the day; at night, it became the romantic meeting place for couples.

The "lovebirds" were walking up-and-down the riverbanks, occasionally crossing a bridge or two, while holding each other's hands, pretending to be a romantically involved couple. At one point, they sat down under one of the beautiful willow trees and tossed pebbles into the water to see who can bounce the pebbles on the water and reach the other side. After awhile, they both find this activity boring and they headed back home.

"So what are we going to do now?" Lacika asked her, it was still too early to go home.

"I know," answered Kati, her face lighted up with an ear-to-ear smile. A casual observer could see the mischief in the eye of this "little rascal" that will get Lacika into trouble. "We are lovers, so we should make love!" The suggestion came from Kati.

"Okay, but how do we do that?" Lacika asked with a puzzled face. He had no clue what was she talking about. The little Lacika at age of six will learn (maybe) something that he did not know before.

"I told you, you do not know anything. I have to teach you everything!" She was angry. "You are just a child. I do not understand what I want from you!"

Let us stop for a second to remind you dear reader, that at the time of the story, Lacika was six and Kati was about eight years old. Kati was talking about sex, making love. Did Kati know what this act was all about it? Certainly, she did not. Was this "real" love? At one point, it was for Lacika! His first lesson started. Sex was a taboo to talk about in those days even for adults. Sex education was not even imagined to be a reality and now an eight-year-old acted as if she was an expert, at least Lacika thought so. She quickly gave Lacika a series of instructions.

"Let us climb up to the attic of the outhouse."

"It must be so dirty there," Lacika pleaded.

"I do not want to hear about it!" she snapped at Lacika. The two kids climbed up to the loft. The "tenants," a flock of pigeons were unhappy seeing the intruders. They were screaming and wildly flapping their wings around in the small low attic until they have found their way out and flew away from the premises. The floor was filled with hardened bird-droppings, the place smelled awful, but these minor inconveniences would not stop the determined Kati.

"Take off your pants and underpants," she ordered, while, she too was taking of her panties. "Sit down, and spread your legs," the instructions continued. Lacika sat down on the dirty floor of the attic, with his bare back. The bird-droppings were hurting his bottom, but he kept his complaints to himself. She also sat down facing him. She too spread her legs apart and crossed them over his legs. They were sitting face-to-face, bottom-to-bottom, very close to each other.

"What do we do now?" Lacika gingerly asked.

"Hm, I am not sure," Kati admitted with a disappointed face.

"Why are we doing this…this thing?" Lacika was puzzled by this whole activity.

"Well, I have seen my sister doing something like this with her boyfriend. I think she liked when they were doing it, otherwise she would not do this most of the time when my parents are not home."

"I think you have to put yours into mine," Kati speculated, but she could figure out how this could be done. She picked up his; she touched hers, but no clue. The situation made both kids frustrated.

"I do not want to do this anymore," Lacika declared. His bottom was really starting to hurt, and what they were doing, did not appear to be any fun anyway.

"Okay, let's go down," Kati agreed with disappointment. By the time they climbed down, it was late in the day and starting to get dark.

"I have to go home, I am going to be in trouble," Lacika said. Indeed, he was in trouble. By the time he arrived home, it was pitch-dark. His worried parents were looking all over for him.

As soon as he got home, Helen angrily asked.

"Where were you? You know you are not supposed to be out after dark."

"I was playing."

"Where did you go? We were looking for you everywhere!" Helen was very angry with her son.

"Somewhere," he was afraid to tell his mother what he was doing. Lacika knew what he was doing was bad, but …

"You are not answering me!" Helen raised her voice. Still, there was no answer from Lacika. Helen lost her temper. She picked up a wooden spoon, grabbed Lacika, and started hitting his behind. This was the first time Helen ever slapped Lacika. He was crying, but still would not divulge his secret.

"No supper for you, young man. You go to sleep and I do not want a word out of you tonight. Tomorrow we will discuss this again."

Lacika went to his bed crying. Not only his bottom was hurting, but also his little heart was hurting even more. He had never experienced this kind of humiliation; nobody ever raised a hand to him before. After awhile, he cried himself to sleep. The next morning, both Ede and Helen tried to explain to Lacika why last night's event was so bad. They were sorry, but they also explained to Lacika that lying and staying out late would not be tolerated in this household.

Most of that morning, he stayed in the house after his parents left for work. By the afternoon, he became restless. After all, he has a "lover" and he could not abandon his object of love, even if their "lovemaking" was unsuccessful.

"Hi, Kati, what are you doing?" Lacika greeted her after he arrived.

"You are late," Kati snapped at him, and then unexpectedly give him a kiss on his mouth. Lacika face became hot and turned all red. He turned around to hide his red face he was genuinely mortified. He was more embarrassed than last night. He had no idea what to do, how to reciprocate.

"Are you going to kiss me back or what?" Kati had sparkles in her eyes from anger. "I thought we are lovers, and this what lovers do!"

"Should I?" Lacika still tried to fight off his redness.

"Sure, we are lovers, aren't we?" Kati quickly stated the facts again. The two embraced and kissed each other on the mouth. Their face turned red and they embarrassedly jumped away from each other. This task was completed and it was over. Lacika was hoping he did not have to do this embarrassing smooching again. His brain and his heart did not agree with each other. He was looking for more "punishment."

"What are we doing today?" Lacika asked, hoping for more exciting things they would do. Actually, he was hoping to go up again to the attic... Well it did not happen.

"We will go to the river again," stated by Kati blocking any possibility of disagreeing with her decision about today's activity. They walked to Stalin Avenue, the main street of the city. Originally, the name of this street was Andrassy Avenue, but like main streets in most towns and cities in Hungary, it was renamed for name of the "great leader" of the Communist world, Comrade Stalin.

This street was lined with stores with large picture windows. The two kids, like many adults, were walking around this street, looking at the store windows, especially the window of the bakery full of appetizing cookies and cakes. They wished to have money for a piece of cake or for an ice cream cone. It was a hot day again. After awhile, they decided to go by the river to cool down. The two were walking a bit and walked back Kati's home. Walking back, Lacika found one Forint in his pocket. Well money usually does not appear in pockets unless someone put it there. Lacika broke into his "savings" to spend it for ice cream, but now he had a girl friend, he wanted to treat her. They stopped at the ice cream store and he asked for two scoops and handed it to Kati. She was surprised, but took it. It was a nice treat. She let him lick the cone occasionally. He was in love!

At the house, Kati noticed that the bicycle of her sister's boyfriend was standing by the house.

"Hey Lacika, want to see what they are doing?" Kati whispered while they were sneaking into the house. They heard noises from the kitchen. Kati and Lacika peeped through the curtains and where not disappointed. They were doing it!

"See what she is doing, you did not do this yesterday." Lacika was expertly analyzing the scene. "She is making those weird noises, you did not do that either."

"See what is he doing, you should have done that." Kati could not leave it without putting in her two cents.

"You seen it before, you should have known what are they doing, when they are doing it." Lacika stopped talking, because it interrupted his concentration. "That is disgusting. Do you see what they are doing?" Lacika said this louder, than he had intended to say. Unfortunately, they both forgot to be quiet and they were discovered. The young man started to chase them and the two kids were screaming and ran outside. They ran into the factory building to hide and were scared to come out for a long time. By the time the two carefully came out, it was already dark.

"I am in real trouble," Lacika yelled to Kati and he sprinted home as fast as he could move his feet. He was right. He was in trouble, again.

"Did we tell you the rules?" Helen screamed at Lacika. "Where were you, again?"

"I was playing."

"Where did you go? What are you doing that is so important that you could not come home on time?" Helen angrily repeated the question.

"Somewhere," he still did not want to tell his mother what he was doing.

"You are repeating the same lies that you told us yesterday," Helen concluded with a shrieking voice. "You will be punished again!" She grabbed the wooden spoon and again she started to pound his behind. Lacika cried hard, he tried to run away from Helen and hide behind the stove, under a chair, but Helen was relentless. She stopped only when the spoon broke.

Lacika never told his parents where he was. Lacika found himself in bed early again and cried until he fell asleep.

§ § § § § §

Neither Helen nor Ede felt good about these events. They did not believe in corporal punishment. Reader, please understand, years ago there were no laws protecting children against an occasional spanking. The general attitude of people was that slapping a kid "could do great deals of good." Parenting never was easy. At times, decisions were made in haste and these decisions sometimes could cause more harm than good. Ede and Helen made a promise; they would never hit Lacika again. They will find a better way to discourage unwanted behaviors.

The next morning, nobody talked about what happened the night before. Helen and as usual Ede went to work. Lacika stayed in the house; he had lots of time to think about the last two days. He simply concluded that women are strange. At this stage in his life, and could be well in the foreseeable future, he does not need the company of a "young woman." He does not need any girl to get him into trouble; he could do this without the "help" of anyone else. He made a "manly" decision not to see Kati ever again, and that was that. He felt much better after this decision. On the other hand, Lacika never forgot his beating in the past two days. It was hard to tell if these beating had anything to do with the fact that Lacika always was considered by others as a "good kid," who respected his parents and most anyone else young or old.

He grabbed a delicious crispy apple and went over to his friends, Sanyi and Misi. After a wonderful day of playing with his friends, he forgot all about Kati.

The idle summer days were running out fast. Fall was approaching fast nothing would stop it. Days started to get shorter and shorter. The sun's rays slowly lost their strengths and one could feel the hot summer already ending. Lacika was over six years old and he was going to start school on the first day of September. Lacika did not know when, but he knew that day would come soon. So far, no one told him about going to school yet.

12

going to school

By now, we know that Ede was an orthodox Jew and he never worked on the Sabbath (Saturdays.) The only time he was forced to work was when he was in the army's Force Labor Service during the war. That time he had no choice. Now he had a choice, his son had a choice too. If someone would have asked Lacika, he might have made a different choice, but nobody asked him; the choice was not his own, it was his father's preference. After all, Lacika was too young to decide his own destiny. You may remember, I mentioned earlier that Ede found in the Hungarian constitution a paragraph that declares that people of Hungary still have religious freedom under the Communist regime. Armed with this weapon, Ede visited the principal of the elementary school. This happened in the early 1950s, when people worked for six days a week and children too attended school for six days a week.

Ede was able to arrange that Lacika would not attend classes on Saturdays! Reader, please forgive me to give away the outcome, but you should not forget that in the early 1950s during the height of the "Stalinist dictatorship," the Communist regulated every aspect of people's lives. The rigid political mentality would not allow immunity from their guiding principles to the non-privileged, everyday people. You also must understand the mentality of these "true believers." The Communists ideology created by these zealots declared that no middle-of-the-road solution exists in their world order. The Communists declared, "If you are not with us, you are against us." No one could take a neutral position. Most of these rules and regulations for the "common people" were not imposed on the "upper echelon," at least while they were on the top. However, if they fell, their privileged position would disappear.

Ede ignored all this gibberish and set out to convince the school principal to make an exception to the general rule. Ede hoped to convince a man who was a devout Communist, a man who got his job because he was a good Communist, and a man who at this time was still a Communist because otherwise, he could not keep this job anymore.

The school principal could not believe his ears when Ede explained his request.

"Comrade Kádár, why do you think that we could grant you this unusual request?" Comrade Szabó stopped for a second and looked at Ede in the eye before he continued.

"All children must attend school on each and every school day, except when they are sick." Comrade Szabó continued his speech with highly noticeable disbelief in his voice and on his facial expressions. "Comrade Kádár, this is the law! There are no exceptions to this rule. How could you even think of this nonsense?"

"Well, I am not asking for something that is illegal. The Constitution of 1949, paragraph 54 clearly affirms the following: 'The Hungarian People's Republic insures the citizens' freedom of conscience and the right of the free practice of any religion.'"

"I am aware of this paragraph," Comrade Szabó quickly replied, but Ede clearly saw on the principal's face that he had never heard of this constitutional law. After a short recovery he continued:

"I still do not believe this applies to your request."

"I understand your concern, Mr. Szabó, but you must understand mine, too." Ede would not call him or anyone else "Comrade." Ede did not sign up for the Communist ideology, he never did. He despised them with a passion. Most of these Communist officials did not like his attitude, but Ede was lucky, most comrades simply ignored his way of addressing people and he rarely got into any trouble for this particular behavior.

"If I could arrange this exception, your son must complete all his schoolwork just like all the other children in the school. We will not give him any slack."

"I perfectly understand that. We will ask one of his classmates that on Saturdays and Jewish holidays to bring home all his homework given by his teachers. I will guarantee that my son will promptly complete all his work assignments."

"Do you know any other kids who may want this kind of exemption?"

"Well, my son is one of the oldest boys in our Jewish community. The Nazis have killed most of our families and our children. I do not have to tell you about all the tragedies that resulted from the horrible acts of the Nazis and the fascists. I know that you are aware of this grief-stricken fact. I suspect that you too may personally have suffered during this unjust war." Ede stopped to observe the principal's face to see if he hit the intended nerve. He did.

"I do know the terrible things the Nazis have done to all of us. This is why we need to fight against the fascists and the capitalists and everyone who is against the working people." His reply was the standard communist line.

"You are right Mr. Szabó. We should fight against all evils." Luckily, Mr. Szabó did not completely understand the distinction that Ede tried to make: fight against all evil would include fighting the Communists too. It was good for Ede's cause, that Comrade Szabó did not understand Ede's hidden message in his comment. Ede would not want to create any animosity with the principal, but this was Ede. The facial expressions of Comrade Szabó told Ede that they agreed on the common cause: fighting against evil.

The psychology seemed to work and the principal continued:

"I cannot make these kinds of decisions. I need to talk to my superiors and I will get back to you."

A few days later Comrade Szabó, sent word that his request was granted. Lacika never attended school on Saturdays or any Jewish holidays while he was attending elementary school. Miki Patakos, a classmate of Lacika who lived a block away, brought home his homework for the next eight years.

§ § § § § §

The school building was built in September 1909 and ever since, it was used for education purposes only. It was a very large and elegant three-story building. Arriving at the main entrance, a visitor would meet a wide marble staircase leading to the upper floors wide enough to allow children and their teachers to go up and down without bumping into each other. Wide hallways connected all the classrooms and labs. All the classrooms had high ceilings, making the room ever more frightening for little children, even though this was not the intentions of the architects. Most classrooms were furnished uniformly. At the front of the room, the blackboard and the teacher's desk were standing on a raised platform providing a better view for the teacher to oversee their students. Facing the teacher's desk there were four rows of student desks. Two kids could sit at each desk. Most classrooms were able to accommodate approximately 40 students. The school had a nice large courtyard where the kids could play and relax between classes. A separate building housed the indoor gym and a large field behind the building was used for all outdoor sport activities.

§ § § § § §

The day has come. Lacika was wearing new pants and a new shirt celebrating the first day of school. He was not too happy to be going to school. He had to get up early in the morning and go to a place where there will be a strange person who will tell him what to do and what not to do. Lacika would no longer be able do his usual daily routines that he had gotten used to ever since he moved in with Ede and Helen. Of course, he got this "inside information" from his older school-aged friends. They should know it well they have been there before.

Lacika was a brave little "man" and did not cry as many other "babies" around him did. On the other hand, he did not understand why his mother was crying. She was not the one who was being left alone with these unfamiliar people in these strange surroundings

I am sure you remember the frightening experience of your first day in school. I think everyone does. Consequently, you could imagine how frightening it was for Lacika. He did not like the fact that during the school day he always had to follow the teacher's instructions. He did not like that most kids in his class were strangers. He did like that there were no girls in his classroom. Even though the school was coed, boys and girls were attending separate classrooms until the fifth grade. He did like that…whatever was associated with the school he did not like.

§ § § § § §

After the Communists took over the government of Hungary, they made numerous changes to the centuries old education system. In the past, the Hungarian education system mostly followed the traditions of the west and mostly adopted the Austrian-German model of schooling. Historically, Hungry was under Germanic influence for centuries. The Hungarian reform movement in the early 19th century and later, following the Austro-Hungarian Compromise of 1867, created an effective education system. A great deal of memorization was part of the current standard teaching philosophy. Memorizing historical facts like dates of events, names, and birthdays of kings and other historical people, mathematic formulas, poems and much other information that sometimes seemed to be completely useless, but according the educators, these will sharpen the children's minds and later in life, these kids will become much better people. Maybe!?

The education systems of yesteryears had something very important that is missing from today's schools. Teachers taught children not only to memorize facts, but also to learn how to think for themselves, and provided tools to find logical solutions to problems. Many world famous scientists would emerge out of the Hungarian education system. Scientists, like John von Neumann, the famous mathematician and father of the computer, like Leo Szilárd, Edward Teller, and Eugene Wigner, who helped to develop the atom bomb, the Nobel laureate Albert Szent-Györgyi, who discovered vitamin C, and many others, too numerous to list.

In reality, during the Communist era, the changes to the fundamental pre-war education system were minimal. Communists forced their political system of belief into every aspect of people's lives, including the education of children and adults, by emphasizing the "fact" that whatever was discovered in science could be explained by the Marxist-Leninist ideology.

In other words, if one understands the communist ideology, one understands the foundations of all scientific disciplines much better. The "Social materialism" was developed by Karl Marx along with Friedrich Engels. The base material of the world (Marx arrived to this conclusion by expanding the Materialism theory) was social relations and mainly class relations between serfs and lord, or today, between employees and employer. The "Social materialism" was an expression of basic social relations and comprised science, economics, law, morality. According to this philosophy adopted by the Communists, every intelligent human being has to understand that God does not exist and everything is based upon the substance of material. Since God does not exist, religion as a belief system has no purpose in anyone's life. The Communist regimes throughout the world tried to conduct people's lives using the above-described philosophy. Does Communism seem like a substitution for traditional religion?

Besides the interjection of communist philosophy into the education system, there were a few other "important" changes implemented. One funny change the new Communist regime implemented was the way students were graded. For centuries, the grading scale of 1 to 5 was used, with one being the best and five the failing grade. For the Communists this kind of grading did not make any sense, and stopped using these "reactionary" old-fashioned practices. I do not have to remind you that for the Communists the "capitalist's ways" were unacceptable. Methods, practices, and behaviors of the capitalists must be modified to serve better the proletariat, the favorite people of the Communists. The education system of the mighty Soviet Union, also adapted this grading method, therefore, if it was good for them it must be equally good for the Hungarian people. Besides, everyone knows that the numerical value of five is higher than the numerical value of one. Therefore, the best grade had to be five (5), for excellence and one (1) should indicate unsatisfactory performance.

§ § § § § §

Lacika had no idea about the above philosophy, teaching methodology, or any other political mumbo-jumbo. He was only concerned about how to survive in this strange environment. The homeroom teacher, Ms. Szalay, was an old teacher who was teaching young kids for over 30 years. Her experience dealing with these frightened kids has helped to ease their fears. On the other hand, she also had to be careful about what she could tell the kids. Her performance was monitored to make sure she supports the current political ideology and guidelines, and would not say anything that could be interpreted as reactionary behavior. Teachers were constantly being "reeducated" by mandatory seminars full of political demagogy. Teachers must be Party members, members of the Communist Party, the only party that was allowed at this time.

The children in the classrooms were seated based upon their height, short ones seated in the front and tall ones in the back. The average height Lacika was assigned to a seat somewhere in the middle of the classroom. The only exceptions to this rule were kids with behavior problems, who were seated in the front of the teacher so the teacher could keep a closer eye on these rascals. Officially, corporal punishment was "discouraged," but an occasional whack with a ruler into the open palm of a guilty child was an acceptable form of punishment. It was used sparingly on the kids with behavior problems.

The schools were run in a semi-military style. As soon as the teacher entered the classroom, the kids would stand up to attention and in unison greeted the arriving teacher:

"Good morning Ms. Szalay."

"Good morning children," the teacher would reply.

Every week, a student-on-duty was appointed by the homeroom teacher to report attendance, to clear the blackboard between classes, and to perform any other chores that the teacher required assistance. After the greetings, the student-on-duty would salute the teacher, and report as follows:

"I, Kiss Miska, am reporting that today everyone is present."

"Thank you, Kiss," the Teacher would reply. "Is there anything else you need to report to me?"

"I am sorry Ms. Szalay, I forgot to mention that today everyone turned in their homework with the exception, and not for the first time, Liptay, who claims that he forgot to bring his homework to school."

"Thank you. Everyone may sit down." After the kids sat down, the teacher opens up the record book that contains all the grades for students in the class. The kids nervously watched the teacher to see who will be called to recite today's homework.

Readers of my age group may remember, but those who are younger might not have experienced the "pleasure" of reciting your homework, in the front of the class, facing your teacher, who would listen carefully to every syllable you were saying, to hit upon anything that may be said incorrectly. Whether you did not study hard, you did not understand the homework, or you were so nervous that you could not get out an intelligent word, the teacher was indifferent to the cause of your mistakes. The teacher did not care for the reason it was not important. The only thing that was important was whether you know or you do not know the homework assignments. Sometimes the teacher may further embarrass you by asking your own peers to correct your mistakes. Your teacher would give you a bad mark, sometimes a failing mark after you were unsuccessful explain your homework correctly in front of the class. Getting a bad mark was not bad enough of a problem, now you had to go home and explain to your parents what happened in class. After dealing with all of this agony, your parents were always on the side of the teacher, and they even have the nerve to tell you:

"You know you deserved it. Why are you complaining? You did not study hard enough! You are punished, you cannot (insert your favorite activity) for a week."

"But mommy, (or daddy) the teacher was picking on me, she hates me, and this was the reason why I got the bad mark."

"Okay, you should know by now that I do not like when you lie to me." Your parent would tell you straight out that, you are wrong with-

out any hesitation. "I know the teacher was right, you did not study."
Now you are starting to be angry, not a good idea, you should know it
better.

"You do not understand me!" Now you scream at your parent; that
was a no-no. You were lucky if you did not get whacked or given further punishment for being dishonest.

Corporal punishment was a common form of punishment from
frustrated parents who did not know how to handle confrontations
with their own children. Most kids were spanked occasionally; it was
a commonly accepted practice. Unfortunately, for many kids in broken homes, child beating was a serious social problem. Many children of this era, coming from families with alcohol addictions, had
serious problems. Government officials were aware of this problem
and intervened once in awhile, but only when situations in these
homes became extremely dangerous for the child. This rampant alco-
holism was well known by the high government officials. If the officials would publicly acknowledge the problem, they were afraid this
problem would provide a source of bad publicity to the west. Nevertheless, all forms of cheap alcohol were available, providing good
income for the same government.

§ § § § § §

It was customary that school aged children were given yearly
checkups by the schools' doctors to discover potential health problems and to give mandatory inoculations to all children. This aspect
of Communism was very positive. During one of these checkups, the
school-doctor would check every child's eyesight. During Lacika's
first checkup, the doctor discovered that Lacika's eyesight was not the
best and he needed glasses. Before he went to school, Ede and Helen
had suspected this problem, but paid little attention to his near-slight-
ness. A few days later, the eye doctor prescribed eyeglasses and from
this day on Lacika wore glasses.

Now, Lacika was seated in the front row so he could see what was
written on the blackboard. His new desk mate was Sanyi Mészáros,
who was sitting there not because of his eyesight, but because his
behavior. He was a nice kid, but in class, he was a menace. Sanyi
could not sit tight, as it was required by the rules. He was talking
while the teacher tried to explain the wonders of mathematics, or to
explain how to write proper sentences, or to appraise the wonderful
life under communism. Sanyi did not pay much attention to all that,
and of course his grades perfectly reflected his attitude. In other

words, he did not do too well in class. Lacika, on the other hand, he was holding his own. He was not one of the best students, but did quite well. As a smart kid, he discovered early in his school years and followed his own philosophy of learning, which he occasionally shared with his friends:

"I could easily be a straight "5" student." Remember five is the best mark.

"So why aren't you?"

"Oh, it takes a lot of work to accomplish that. I would have to study hard every single day; I do not want to study hard."

"Why not?"

"Because when I am considered as a good student, maintaining the average marks of four, the teachers would not expect me to do well all the time. This way, I could demonstrate my occasional "brilliance" in front of teachers and fellow students, and make it noticeable for everyone how much I do know. To show everyone that I am so smart had always been very exciting!"

Well, Lacika had some argument from his father about this philosophy. Ede was claiming, and many times proving, he was a good student in his own days. He was proud of his Latin knowledge and many times used Latin proverbs to prove his point, such as:

"Lacika you must understand, as the Latin proverb said: "Non scholae, sed vitae discimus.—We learn not for school but for life.""

The Hungarian economy was not getting any better, shortages of basic goods was making people's lives miserable, uncomfortable. The cold winter of 1951 was colder for many citizens because of shortages of firewood and coal. People had to use their rationing coupons to obtain their allotment for many necessities. Even people, who had the money to buy coal to heat their apartment, could not get enough due to shortages of supply. The Kádár family was not immune to the shortage. To conserve coal and wood, they moved into the small laundry room since it could be kept warm using less fuel than the large bedroom would require. Two couches and a convertible sofa provided their sleeping accommodations. When the sofa was opened at night, the three pieces filled the room wall-to-wall leaving only enough room at the other end of the room for an iron stove and a small table. It was incredibly tight accommodations for three people. When Helen was cooking, the cooking stove warmed up the kitchen so the family was eating in the kitchen. Otherwise, they spent their time in the laundry room that they used as a combination living, dining, and bedroom of less than 15 square meters (160 square feet.) The rest of the house was freezing cold. Might as well be, the bathroom in the house was unusable anyway. Some of the pipes inside the walls were leaking. The housing authority that owned the villa after the nationalization, would not fix it. Why should they? Most people did not have running water in their houses in the neighborhood. Why should the Kádár family have the comfort of running water? The workers shut down the well, and drinking water was no longer available. Of course, this made the toilet almost unusable, since water did come into the house to flush the toilet. Well, the Kádár family still was using the inside toilet. They used water stored in a large container to flush. They got the water from the non-drinking water well which still working in the courtyard. Sometimes, it was so cold in this part of the house that the stored water would freeze in the winter. To get drinking water, people were carrying handheld jugs to carry water from the nearest artesian well, a few blocks away. Ede would not spend any money to fix the plumbing problem, because he felt that this house was not his house anymore so why should he spend any money on it. It was hard to understand why he refused to renovate. After all, spending some money on his residence would make the life of his family a bit better. It must have been his anger toward the government was so strong that he completely ignored reality. This house would be his home for many years to come. The Kádár family lived in this house until the spring of 1966. Their apartment had no running water between 1951 and 1963, when the city finally brought running water to the neighborhood.

The first year of school passed without any particular events worth mentioning with the exception that unfortunately Lacika was frequently sick during the first school year and almost every other school year. His parents had to go to work. Therefore, Lacika was staying home alone when he was sick and could not go to school. Helen gave him instructions on what to do, when to take medications, when to eat lunch, when to stay in bed, and when to get up. It was not as bad as it is sounds. He liked being alone. He always found a way to keep busy with some activity so he was rarely bored.

Lacika experienced various types of sicknesses, but nothing too serious. He was very fragile and susceptible to illnesses like various forms of chickenpox, whooping cough, flu, rashes of all kinds, and severe headaches. Who could remember them all? Helen tried everything to ease his pain and suffering using medicines of all kinds including home remedies like "Chicken soup," and "old wives' tale" superstition cures. Helen was using one of the most ridiculous treatments for his headaches. This "cure" came from her family in Nagy-dobos. Since in Helen's eyes Lacika was a beautiful child, as a result, people envied him and therefore they gave him "ayin hara" (evil eye). Her "cure" was to dump burning wood-charcoal into cold water. This brew had to be swallowed by Lacika. Did this cure ever work? I do not know, but the headaches went away eventually and, if nothing else, it was a memorable experience.

§ § § § § §

Summer was finally here and Lacika had his first summer vacation. He was so happy about staying in bed as long as he wanted, no more studying, no more homework, and he did not need to do anything. In the hot summer days, he was running around, as many other kids did in those days, barefooted and wearing a black short without a shirt. He would play with his friends in the neighborhood all day, playing without a care in the world. These were happy days for Lacika. His parents were working during most of the day. The long daylights of the summer would give Helen and Ede more time to spend with Lacika. Helen was cooking in most of her "spare" time. Her baking was wonderful and simple; Lacika loved her cookies. These cookies were always available and Helen was happy that Lacika was eating them. She was hoping that Lacika would gain some weight, since he was so skinny and fragile. On the front of his pants there was a large pocket which he would fill with cookies before would run out to play. He was a nice boy and the whole neighborhood was eating Helen's cookies until Helen discovered where all those cookies went. She really did not mind, but they could not afford to feed everyone in the neighborhood. Helen carefully had to explain to Lacika that sharing is very nice, but there is a limit to how much he should share.

In those days, most people were not familiar with the idea of television in Hungary until the early sixties, and even then, the majority of families could not afford to buy one. Unlike today, when kids are spending enormous amounts of time front of the TV, kids in the fifties had to find other activities to pass their time. You must know that I am not a philosopher, but living through the fifties, I do remember how long a 24-hour day felt like. Let me count the hours.

Of course, we were sleeping more or less for 8 hours, I slept more, but this is not important. The remaining 16 hours or so still constitute a long time. Let us assume that we had three square meals a day and some snacks in between, which may reduce the day by another two hours. That leaves us still 14 hours to kill. During the school year, the time would be reduced by the amount of time spent attending classes and completing our homework. The schools were opened between 7:00 and 7:30 and kids were let out between 12:00 noon and 2:00 PM depending on the grade a child was attending. Ok, the length of a day was reduced between 5 and 7 hours. After we went home, our mothers were serving us the main meal of the day, a hearty freshly cooked lunch. Most mothers stayed home and did not need to work outside of the house. Following a brief playtime, homework must be completed.

The homework assignments were much more intensive than my American children ever had. We were not allowed to complain about it. My father always quoted the Latin phrase: "Non scholae sed vitae discimus." (We do not learn for the school, but for life.) Meaning: do not bother me with your complaints, study hard and you will find a better life in the future. Working hard is a prerequisite for a successful future.

After finishing the daily assignments: homework and study the day almost was over and it was time to go to bed early, the next day will start early. You would think Sundays and holidays were worry free days. Sorry you are wrong. Teachers were telling us that on non-school days, you have nothing better to do, so, you should do something useful. They assigned us more homework than on weekdays. By the way, during the summer vacation numerous book-reading assignments were given to us with the same explanation. "It is a long summer, do something useful like reading War and Peace from Leo Tolstoy." Have you ever read this huge two-volume book and written a book report on your summer vacation?

The summertime was different for Lacika from other boys of his age. Helen and Ede would not let him go to summer camps for two reasons. The most important reason was that kosher food was not available at the camps. In those days, no Jewish camps existed in Hungary. These summer camps were used mostly for political "education" of the children, to show the children how much the Communist government values the new generation. Of course, the hidden agenda was to reinforce their minds with the Communist demagogy and build up their body's strength for the hard work they will face in the future. True, everyone gained something. The children had much fun being there and the government groomed their future leaders.

Lacika was busy during the day regardless. There were many kids in the neighborhood to kick a football (soccer); to run around; to play sometimes-silly games; to get into a fight with your best friend and many other "wonderful" activities that a laid-back summer day would provide. Across the street from the house, there was a large empty lot which neighborhood kids called a "park." Well, during the war, a misguided bomb leveled some houses and the city decided not to build any new ones to replace them. They cleared out the rummage and nature did its share to provide some grass and other plants to make the area somewhat pleasant. In later years, they even planted some trees to make it more like a park. Sometimes, some building materials stored in one area of the "park" made it somewhat unsafe to play there, but with the exceptions of some cuts-and-bruises, no one ever endured any serious injuries.

A rarely used railroad track separated the street and the park. Occasional trains going by had given some dangerous excitement for the local kids, such us running across and along the moving train triggering a nervous set of whistles from the conductor. Walking on the rails pretending it is high-wire act would also add some activity to pass time in a long summer day. Talking about high-wire acts reminds me of the highlight of the summer for Lacika: the CIRCUS.

The empty lot had more than sufficient space to pitch a large circus tent and park all the trailers. In the morning, circus clowns, musicians, beautiful young (and sometimes not so young or so beautiful) women in exotic daring dresses, and circus animals, mostly horses, elephants, and dogs dancing on their hind legs would parade down from the railroad station. They would play loud music to attract people's attention for the show that would come that night. This sight made all kids hearts beat a little bit faster. For a free pass to the show, the circus would hire older kids to help pitch the tent. Lacika would also join the fun of running around among the circus personnel. At night, he would go to see that show with his parents. They always sat in the last top row. Helen would encourage Lacika to stand up on the seat to see everything better, and Helen always told Lacika this was the reason why they were sitting so high. She never mentioned the real reason: these seats were the cheapest. Lacika did not care since he was enjoying the show. Sometimes, there was an early show, which Lacika rarely missed; he managed to sneak in through the back of the tent to see the show again.

On one summer day, Lacika had a frightening, but exciting experience at the circus. Ede somehow knew the lion-tamer working at one of the circuses visiting Békéscsaba. Ede introduced the trainer to Lacika. Lacika was about 10 years old. The lion-tamer was explaining how he trains these "fearsome beasts." He told some of his secrets to his guests. He obtained these lions when they were little cubs and, like kittens, they would learn to love their owners. True, these animals were wild and they could never truly be tamed 100 percent. He explained to Lacika that these animals could sense if someone was afraid of them and this would encourage them to be aggressive toward that person. At one point, the lion-tamer climbed into the lion's cage and illustrated how to approach the lion. He jokingly said to Lacika:

"I have just fed these kittens; they will not eat you, why don't you come in?"

"No, no, no," he exclaimed, "I cannot do that!"

"Why are you so afraid? I am here and I will protect you, if needed."

"I will not go in there; they have sharp teeth and sharp nails."

"Don't worry, this old beast hardly have any teeth left." He went over to the lion and opened his mouth to illustrate. Well, she had some teeth, but not too many and they did not looked so sharp. Lacika took a deep breath and went into the cage, his face turned white, and he was fighting off his shivering.

"Come closer and stroke his head. Make sure that when you approach the lion do not hesitate, go for it with conviction."

"No way," Lacika whispered.

"I am telling you, there is nothing to fear." Finally, Lacika made his move stroke the lion's mane. The large cat just sat there with his sad eye glancing at him for a second and then put his head on his paws completely ignoring Lacika.

"See I told you," said the man "There is nothing to it." Lacika was glad to exit from the cage. He was proud of his adventure and courage, but never again would he go back to meet a lion face-to-face like this.

By night, Lacika was filthy beyond belief from head to toes. He got into everything as if he was searching for places where one could get the "best filth" ever. Helen was joking about his son for years to come. She had to use rubbing alcohol to clean him up every night. Since the bathroom was unusable, the unwelcomed nightly bathing was performed using a bucket filled with water, sometimes with cold water. A washcloth and soap was used to go over every part of Lacika's body until he was clean. Helen had a hard time combing his hair, because Lacika had such stringy hair that would never stay where Helen wanted it to stay. Many broken combs were the witnesses of Helen's losing battle with the stubborn hair of Lacika.

Lacika loved summer. By the end of the summer, he looked like a gypsy. His skin became dark, suntanned from spending all day under the hot summer sun. Sometimes Helen jokingly complained that she could not distinguish if it was dirt or it was his tan that, she was trying to wash off from Lacika's skin.

13
another setback

It would be a miracle, if life under the Communist regime would be without any hardships. Why should the lives of everyday people be eventless? People just wanted to survive and live a peaceful existence in this harsh, trying era. The head of households, mostly men, want to provide a decent existence for the family. Most people did not care about politics. The communist leadership wanted people to "support" the current regime; they wanted everyone to join "the PARTY," the only political party they allowed. The official name for the Communist party did not contain the word "Communist," the official name was the "Hungarian Working People's Party" (MDP—Magyar Dolgozók Pártja). The name suggested that the Working People were in charge, but it was not the case. The leaders like Mátyás Rákosi and his designated successor Ernő Gerő were in charge. An interesting fact is that these two both were born to Jewish parents. The people under their influence interfered with the lives of the masses to save their own hide, "big brother" was watching.

Officials from the lower levels to upper levels of the Communist party had to show to their bosses that their trust was appreciated. They had to prove that any low-level bureaucrat could to do something "constructive" for the party for the further good of the working proletariats, the working masses.

The political situation in Hungary was changing after Stalin died in March 1953. The new Soviet leadership soon permitted a more flexible policy in Eastern Europe known as the "New Course." In June, Mátyás Rákosi and other party leaders were summoned to Moscow, where Soviet leaders harshly criticized them for Hungary's miserable economic performance. Rákosi was chastised for naming so many Jews to Hungary's top party positions and accused him of seeking to

make himself the "Jewish King of Hungary." In Hungary, communists of Jewish origin had dominated the party leadership and the
secret police for a decade after the war. Rákosi retained his position as
party chief, but the Soviet leaders forced the appointment of Imre
Nagy as prime minister, ended the purges, and began freeing political
prisoners. In his first address to the National Assembly as prime minister, Nagy attacked Rákosi for his use of terror and the speech was
printed in the party newspaper.

Nagy planed his "New Course" for Hungary's drifting economy.
Hungary ceased collectivization of agriculture, allowed some peasants to leave the collective farms, canceled the collective farms' compulsory production quotas, and raised government prices for
deliveries. Government financial support was extended to private producers and peasants were able to increase the size of their private
plots. The number of peasants on collective farms thus shrank by half
between October and December 1953. Nagy also slashed investment
in heavy industry, shifting resources to light industry and to the production of consumer goods. However, Nagy failed to alter the planning system or to introduce new incentives to replace compulsory
plan targets set, resulting in worse production records after 1953 than
before. Rákosi used his influence to disrupt Nagy's reforms and erode
his political position. After Nagy's fall, collectivization and development of heavy industry again became the prime focus of Hungary's
economy. The purges did not resume, however, as Rákosi did not
enjoy the same amount of power or Soviet support that he did while
Stalin was alive.

§ § § § § §

You may remember Comrade Kocsis, who was interrogating Ede
when he was taken away for gun possession. Comrade Kocsis could
never get over his failure to make Ede confess something that would
incriminate himself. He kept his eye on Ede ever since he was
released. He noted that Ede was doing well and in the meantime,
Comrade Kocsis was still stuck in the county jail in Gyula interrogating political prisoners, he was sick of this job already.

Comrade Kocsis did not like Jews, and the changing attitudes of
the communist leadership towards Jews gave him additional ammuni-
tion to do something to enhance his stagnant career. He was hoping
his brilliant plan would get Ede into trouble again. He convinced, or
rather forced, one of the workers at the Waste Processing Company to
become his eyes and ears. As the standard job of a mole, he would

watch and listen to everything that was said by his coworkers and kept careful notes about them. He was instructed to report everything that was happening in the factory to Comrade Kocsis. Comrade Kocsis would carefully analyze every piece of information to find something that he could interpret as reactionary and could lead to actions to harm the "establishment."

By this time, the Waste Processing Company was operating smoothly. Good-looking products produced by its workers were appearing on store shelves and people were buying them. The business venture was a success. As we know, people are always jealous of others who succeed. The workers at the Waste Processing Company did not suspect anything. They had no clue that they were being spied on. They should have though; it was the "standard" practice of the communist tyranny. Comrade Kocsis slowly collected "evidence" until he was ready to present his case. With all his "evidence' on hand, he walked into the office of his superior Comrade János Hajdú. They had known each other for a long time, so Comrade Kocsis was sure that Comrade Hajdú would be open to his presentation.

János had sobered up somewhat, drinking a few drinks would not be labeled being an alcoholic in those days; it was considered good social behavior. János found his destiny, became a "true believer." He fabricated a fictitious history where he suffered a great deal as a Communist sympathizer before the war. He was not well educated, but he was smart and he understood what to do to succeed in the new era. Slowly, he moved up in the Communist party ranks and he was appointed to a regional level bureaucrat.

"Good morning Comrade, it has been awhile since I saw you last." János greeted Comrade Kocsis with wide smile on his face. He got up from his desk and gave him a big hug and a kiss on both cheeks as good brothers of the mighty Communist Party usually would.

"I am happy to see you. I am sorry I did not call upon you until now, but I am very busy at the county jail. There are so many of these despicable people still around who want to destroy our great proletariat state."

"Would you like to have an espresso coffee or a shot of plum brandy?" the host offered his guest. These amenities were always available for higher-level bureaucrats.

"Thank you, I take a coffee."

"Mariska, get us two coffees!" János jelled out to his secretary. A few minutes later, a cute attractive blond walked in with a tray filled with some cookies and two cups of steaming espresso coffee. The two men talked more about old times while they ate some cookies and drank their coffee.

This kind of chitchat was an obligatory routine when true communists were talking to each other in an office environment making sure that whoever listens (yes, someone was listening, spying at all times even if they were not, one would not take any chances,) to their discussion would know for sure they were "good" comrades. Most government and many non-government offices were bugged. Most people working in government offices knew about the listening devices. If they wanted to talk in "private," they would go outside or go to a café or restaurant. Even some people's homes were bugged.

"How can I help you?" János stopping this short reminiscing. He was ready get to the serious business part of the visit.

"I am sure that you know Ede Kádár." Comrade Kocsis started his mission. "You also know that he is managing the Waste Processing Company with about 40 employees. You also know..." he stopped for a second, looked around hoping for privacy, and whispered, "He is Jewish." He made a face showing an expression of disgust, expecting a similar reaction from János who was sitting there without a word, without any reaction.

"Hmm, this is not a good sign," Comrade Kocsis thought, but boldly continued:

"Are you aware of what kind of people he employs? They are representing the capitalists that we all fighting against. They are ALL enemies of our wonderful Proletariat state. These are the kinds of people, who poisoned our lives in the past. They were treating us poor working people badly, why should we better their lives?" Comrade Kocsis stopped talking. The expected approval from Comrade Hajdú did not materialize. Not a beep was heard from János. Comrade Kocsis was confused. What could he have said wrong? How come this information did not make his comrade excited? Maybe he already knows all about it. This must be it!

The two men were sitting there quietly for a while. They both hesitated to continue the discussion, suspecting each was building a trap for the other. One never knew these things could happen to anyone at anytime. Setting traps was fair play. Finally, János break the silence.

"Is there anything concrete you can tell me or are all these allegations are a fiction of your imagination?

"Absolutely." Comrade Kocsis came alive. "I conducted some research on most of the workers. These people are reactionaries. Let me tell you about some of them. Arthur Greenberg used to be the owner of the two-story building on Stalin Avenue; the first floor was his wholesale business and upstairs was his apartment. Today there are four families living comfortably in that apartment. He was exploiting about 25 workers giving those minimum living wages while he was making millions."

"Miksa Kohn owned the Brick factory in Jamina, employing hundreds hard working men. These poor people were working 10 to 12 hours a day while he was vacationing in his private villa in Abbazia (Opatija) by the Adriatic Sea."

"Jacob Rosenthal's father owned the István steam-mill that was nationalized in 1946 and ever since we, the working people, proudly own it. It provides a great service to our economy and the owner could no longer take advantage of our hard working honest workers. We are helping these people to make a good living and allow them privileges beyond the privileges of everyday people."

"Simon Weisz owned numerous businesses. One of them was an import business where he was selling farm products to Austria, paying minimum wages to our hard working farmers, while he owned many beautiful houses here in Békéscsaba and a huge vacation villa by the Lake Balaton."

"I could go on and on. All the information I have collected is in this folder." He handed János a big folder. "We must do something about this. You know they are working on Sunday, and not on Saturday. How can we allow this? They are against all of us. I had an informer planted in and all their incrementing conversations were documented."

János now started to pay attention to this "gold-mine" of information. He really did not care about these people's working habits, their past, and what did they were doing years ago. He was only interested in furthering his own career.

"OK, Comrade Kocsis, or rather my friend Józsi, I will look over everything you gave me and I will get back to you shortly." János stood up, signaling the end of the meeting. János was excited and was more than ready to take the next step to start a new chapter in his career.

§ § § § § §

It was 5:00 o'clock in the afternoon, right before the end of the workday. Ten policemen and two plain-clothed secret service men busted into the building of the Waste Processing Company. Using a hand-held loudspeaker, they told everyone to immediately get up from their workstations, leave the building, and wait in the court-yard. For Jews this scene was scary, it reminded them days not long ago with the Nazis. They were panicking, some women were crying. The police were acting calm and they did not harm anyone, but firmly directed workers to leave the factory building. Comrade Hajdú was in charge and using his loudspeaker, started to talk to the employees:

"The leadership of the Party will no longer allow you to work in this facility. We, the strong supporters of the Communist ideology, feel this place has become a meeting place for people who are against our values and we do not want to support your reactionary behavior. As of now, you are all free to go home, please take all your personal belongings, and leave the premises within 15 minutes. Make sure that whatever belongs to us, the working-people, leave behind and take only what belongs to you."

Considering the way this situation turned out, it was unusually for-giving to people who were considered intransigent, imperialist or "enemy of the state." They were all lucky that nobody was arrested for some trumped up charges, especially Ede, who had his share of troubles. Someone must have been looking after his wellbeing, maybe, no one would know this for sure.

After everyone, including Helen and Ede, finished packing up their belonging, like thieves they all quietly disappeared one by one, leav-ing behind an eerily quiet, empty building. The police locked up, sealed the building, and hanged a large sign on the door:

UNDER GOVERNMENT CONTROL
NO ENTRY
‡‡‡‡‡
Anyone entering these premises
will be punished by law

The courtyard had become quiet, for days no one would dare to come by. Ex-employees were afraid to visit the synagogue or go to the slaughtering house. They were all afraid that their action might trigger some "punishment."

Ede was devastated. For the last few years, his life seemed stable and he was more or less happy. He had a son, he had a lovely wife, and he was able to provide a decent life for his family. He hated the establishment, the idea of communism, and the people who ran the "new and better way of life." He was afraid to criticize the new gov-ernment, and the people who ran the government openly. In one day, he lost his stable existence, and again, he found himself without any means of providing for his family. What could he do? Well, for days he did not do anything. Maybe for the first time in his life, he felt helpless, depressed, and devastated. He would sit on the couch staring into the open air without any expression on his face. Helen was scared. She had never seen her husband in this state of mind, even during the worst of the Holocaust. She had to do something to get Ede moving, and do something, to come to life, become himself again.

"What are you thinking about?" Helen tried to start a conversation, no answer.

"Is there anything I can do to help? Are you sick? Should I call a doctor?" It was like talking to the wall.

"Did I do something wrong, are you mad at me?" He would not answer or talk to her or anyone else. This was so uncharacteristic of Ede that Helen started to cry uncontrollably. There was absolutely no reaction from Ede. This horror went on for days. He hardly ate anything and did not even smoke one cigarette for several days. For a heavy smoker, not to smoke under normal circumstances would be intolerable. It was strange, but he did not touch a single cigarette.

Lacika was scared, too. He did not understand his father's behavior. Lacika got accustomed to see his father as a man with a mission, a man who was always talking to everyone and always telling interesting stories of his life. Like a story from when he was in the army. The stories went like this:

One of my subordinates, Mr. Cohn, requested a furlough. I have to tell you, sometimes, you have watch out for our Jewish brethrens, or they will swindle you blind.

"Moshe, why do you want to go home now? I asked the man.

"You know lieutenant, my wife is confined to bed, and I need to visit her."

"Ok, then I will grant you a vacation tomorrow for two weeks." I generously decided to give this poor man time to visit his sick wife. Mr. Cohn came back after the two weeks were over and I ask him:

"How is your wife, is she OK?"

"Yes she is, but why do you ask?" Let me tell you, he had the guts to ask me this question. Can you believe this chutzpah?

"You told me the she was "bedridden" and I was worried about your wife, because I thought she was sick."

"You must have misunderstood me, she is fine now, and she was fine then. Some Good Samaritan gave us a bed with a mattress. We are poor and could not afford a normal bed. We were sleeping on a sack filled with hay. I had to go home to try out our new bed! It is very comfortable to sleep in it."

§ § § § § §

Lacika was sad seeing his father like this. His father was silent. No more stories were being told. He did not act the way his father usually behaved.

"Hey Daddy, what is going on?" Lacika screamed at him. Ede did not even look at him; he was staring at something that no one could see.

"Why don't you talk to me? Please let us play something together, as we usually do. Daddy, can you speak?" Nothing was said. "Are you playing some game with me?" Lacika started to smile, but the smile was gone fast. After all this, his father was still motionlessly sitting on his chair.

"Mommy, what is wrong with Daddy? Why won't he talk to me?"

"I do not know, I think he is sick!" Helen answered with little or no conviction in what she was saying. Helen did not know what to do. As a last resort, Helen went to see the Rabbi for advice. Mr. Schnitzler was also lost for words hearing about Ede's state of mind. He could not believe that his friend Ede could be like this. He tried to comfort Helen:

"I could understand what Ede is feeling. He has tried to do the right things, but he certainly feels he failed." Rabbi Schnitzler talked to Helen in his usual smoothing voice. As a Rabbi, he developed a way of conversing with his followers. His mannerism did provide the people with some feeling of comfort, some feeling of hope for the future. "I will go and visit you shortly and I will try to talk to Ede. With the help of G-d everything will be good."

Helen walked home. Her feet felt so heavy that she had to drag them as if they filled with rocks. The short ten-minute walk home felt like hours passed. She could not shake off her bad feeling even after hearing the kind words of Rabbi Schnitzler. She was religious, but lately religion did not give her the comforting hope for better future as she felt in the past. She has in extremely rare occasions talked about her deportation days, as if she pretended that it never happened. She saw again and again that they have tried to be righteous, tried to be good people, but it seemed that lately G-d had turned away from the Kádár family. As she was walking home lost in her thoughts, did not notice anything or anybody. She walked by her good friend, the wife of Béla Bánki, Edna without realizing her presence.

"Hello Helen, You don't even see me? Is anything wrong, you look depressed?"

"Hi, I am sorry I truly did not see you Edna." Helen was embarrassed about not noticing her friend. "I am sure you heard what happened to our factory. Ede is acting strange; I do not know what to do."

"Yea, I did hear about it, but we too do not understand what happened. You know, Béla is not home. He had to attend some meeting or seminar in Budapest and he will not be back for a couple of weeks. It is bad for me with the two kids alone, without any help." Edna had this "habit" of talking a mile-a-minute not paying any attention to the other party. She realized she was taking too much and apologized:

"I am sorry Helen, I was rude. I know your problem is much worse than my petty issues. Since my husband is not around, I could not even try to suggest anything to help you."

"Thank you, I do know you guys are always there for us. Would you like to come over for coffee? Ede may be happy to see you, but if he is not, please forgive him."

"It would be lovely." The two women walked to Helen's home.

"Hello Ede, how are you?" Edna greeted Ede, who was mumbling something under his nose, and did not get up as he usually would to welcome a friend. Edna understood the situation and the two women went into the kitchen for their coffee. They were talking for a while until Ede appeared in the doorway.

"The coffee smells good, can I get some?" The two women look at each other without a word. Helen poured a cup and offered a piece of cake. Ede took it, turned around, and left with the food without saying another word.

"See what is happening? Today he said a few words, unlike the way he was behaving lately. I guess he likes you!" Helen tried to make light of the situation. The doorbell was ringing. Helen opened the door, and to her surprise, Rabbi Schnitzler appeared in the opening. Helen did not know how to react and yelled:

"Ede! Ede! Mr. Schnitzler is here to see you."

"Rabbi Schnitzler, please do not tell him that I was visiting you," Helen whispered to the Rabbi. He nodded with a smile.

"Shalom Aleichem, Mr. Kádár," he greeted Ede with a respectful voice. "I have not seen you in shul on Shabbat. Are you feeling well?" "Aleichem Shalom," Ede answered with the customary greeting. "I am sure you know what has happened to us. I am scared. What would the communist do to me again? It may not be a good idea for you to visit me. I do not think they like you either. They would use anything against us to make our life even more miserable."

"I am aware of all this, but we Jews must stand up for each other in any situation. You have to remember what happened during the war! We Jews were fighting with each other, and as a result, we lost our communities. We must help each other, we should not worry about the potential danger that may come upon us because we all bound together to help each other. We must be diligent and resilient. Our strength must come from our unity and we will prevail."

"What can I do? I feel that I have made a grave mistake staying in this G-d forsaken country. I should have left, like many did," Ede answered with bitter, angry voice.

"You forget one important thing: G-d works in mysterious ways. Have you forgotten Lacika, your son? What would have happened to him if G-d did not direct your life to Békéscsaba? Our community would have one less member, one less Jewish child to build our future. This was your mitzvah. This was your doing, this was your destiny."

"I understand what you are saying, but how many disappointments can one man endure in a lifetime? For the first time in my life, I am lost. I do not know what to do." Rabbi Schnitzler stopped for few second and continued:

"The good book says: G-d will help those who would help them self. Ede, you must put yourself together and do something to help your family. You cannot sit here to wait for a miracle. It is your responsibility, as a husband, as a father, to take care of your family. A man of your caliber could do anything, and you have proved this time after time in the past. I am sure that G-d will open your eyes to see clearly. He will open your eyes to see the road that will lead you to your future, and you will succeed."

"It is getting late, and I need to go to the evening prayer service. Would you join me, Ede?" Rabbi Schnitzler was getting ready to leave, and unbelievably, Ede went with him to shul for the first time in many weeks. The two men walked silently, both enthralled by their own deep thoughts. Ede started to realize that the Rabbi was right;

doing nothing would harm his family. He must establish some kind of work where he could keep the Sabbath and still earn enough money to support his family.

Ede recalled desperate times during the war when he served in Forced Labor Service as a lieutenant when he found the way to survive. This story is one of the stories Lacika heard and cherished every time Ede was telling anyone who would be willing to listen to it.

> *"My unit as part of the Hungarian Second Army, ended up near the bend of river Don, where the Hungarian military had its worst defeat ever from the Red Army (approx 140,000 dead and wounded.) After this bloody battle, the remainder of the Hungarian army was retreating, or rather was running away from the Russians in disastrous disarray. My squadron was also ordered to retreat. Of course, the Hungarians would not give any supplies to us Jews and to the other undesirable people. How could I escort back my people, my fellow Jews, to safety without any transportation, food and other necessities? One after another, my requests for supplies were refused by the Hungarians I had to do something. As you know, I speak perfect German. What could I lose? I approached the nearest German supply depot and requested to be supplied with some food and other things. The Germans were allies with the Hungarian, they did not know about us, the Forced Labor Service; I was wearing my lieutenant uniform, and they gave me all that we requested. I guess, I had the guts, and I succeeded in saving many poor souls from certain death from the harsh Russian winter."*

Ede was thinking about his own story and made a decision: nothing lost; he will find the way to go forward for his family and for the community.

14

there is a way out!

Ede had only a few options for his future endeavors. Moving to Budapest would give him an opportunity to work for the Central Jewish Administration (CJA) in hope that they would offer some kind of a job for an orthodox Jew. Neither Helen nor Ede was fond of the life in Békéscsaba, but they were not sure if they would like the hustle-and-bustle of the large city life any better. Besides, it was close to impossible to get permission to establish residence in the over-crowded capitol city of Hungary. First, a temporary residence had to be established for people working in Budapest. Renting a single room offered by some families to supplement their income was the only alternative, and Ede would not accept this for his family. Renting an apartment was virtually impossible due to the severe housing short-age in the 1950s. He could ask the Jewish organization to allow them to live in one of their apartments, but Ede did not have any connec-tions to get one. This avenue was dead even before they seriously considered it. He did not choose this possibility mostly because Ede did not like the way the CJA organization was run. Ede historically never had a good relationship with them. Maybe as a last resort, but for now he had to find a local work opportunity.

After finishing the evening prayer, Ede stopped by Uncle Yayli as he has done many times in the past. They were very good friends. The two men started to talk about what are their hopes for the future. Ede seen a hopeless future for his family, until Uncle Yayli, with his most matter-of-fact tone of voice, said:

"Why can't we continue operating the Remnants and Waste Recov-ery Company?"

"How can we do this?" Ede replied with a voice of disbelief. "The government seized the building and forbid us to work there." Ede stopped talking without expecting any reasonable answer from Uncle Yayli, but Uncle Yayli did not give up and continued his train of thought.

"Why can't we work from home? If we work at home, then the Government would not know or care about which days we work on." Uncle Yayli, with his simplistic mind, came up with a great solution.

"Thank you, you are great!" Ede jumped up from his seat.

"How do I deserve this appraisal? What was I was saying, that you do not know already?"

"You are so smart! You gave me the perfect idea how to continue our way of life without compromise. Tomorrow, I will talk to Mr. Katz and we will start working on your suggestion." Ede got energized, and with his usual brisk walk, went home. He hugged Helen, kissed her on her cheek, and said:

"Helen dear, I think we have solved our unemployment problem." He had a big smile on his face. Helen was happy to see her husband well again. Wasting no time, the next day Ede went to see his friend, Jenő.

"Hello my friend," Mr. Katz greeted Ede, when he walked into his office. "What brings you here? Don't tell me you have another idea."

"Good morning to you!" Ede said. He had a big smile on his face and a twinkle in his eyes. "How did you guess?"

"Well I heard about what happened a few weeks ago and I know you must find employment, so what do you want to tell me?"

"You are absolutely right. I need you again. Interestingly enough, this was not my idea. You do know Uncle Yayli; he came up with the idea. We should all work from home. Instead of getting an hourly rate, workers would be paid for each piece they produce. This way, they can work any day, any time and as many hours as they want to work. This is why I am here."

"It is a great idea. My bosses are already complaining that we have missed the last few shipping dates. The people at the State Department Store are wondering about when the next shipment would be arriving in their warehouse. Our products became very popular."

"So, what do we need to do?"

"I will present this idea to my bosses in Budapest. I think they will probably send someone here who could analyze the manufacturing process. Based upon the analysis, they will calculate how much to pay for each piece so our employees would earn a reasonable income."

"I will talk to the ex-workers to see who would be willing to work from home. Jenő, please start contacting your bosses."

"By the way," Ede continued, "your bosses need to make some inquires about the already finished products that were locked in the factory building. They should find a legal way to get everything back to us, assuming anything is still there. In addition, we need to get all the equipment: metal stamps, sewing machines and everything else that was left in the factory when it was shut down. We will need them for the future production."

"You are right! I did not think of this. Do not worry, Ede, I will take care of it all. After all, that equipment is the property of this factory."

In the following few days Ede visited all the people who had worked in the Remnants and Waste Recovery Company and told them his plan and encouraged them all to continue working for him. Unfortunately, many ex-workers did not have large enough apartments where they would be able to continue working. Out of the original 45 employees, only 19 signed up. The good news for Ede was that he would be gainfully employed, assuming the "upper management" would give the go-a-head to continue the production. The not-so-good news was that the production would be greatly reduced until Ede could hire more people.

It was frustrating to wait. The bureaucrats have their way to slow down progress. The Central headquarters in Budapest been challenged to figure out the process for pricing piecemeal or rather, calculate the amount of pay that would considered a reasonable living wage for an individual. How could an average hourly rate be calculated based upon an 8-hour workday for people working at their own pace? How could an average hourly rate be calculated based upon production volume? How could these individual workers earn a salary that would be comparable to other workers? Finally, a somewhat logical formula was created. They will send a person who would watch each step of the production, and time the number of pieces produced per hour. The average hourly rate will be divided by the number of pieces produced by each worker. After all points of view were discussed, the solution was simple.

The word come that the person was coming next week, and Ede started to organize the demonstrations so the process will be smooth. He also hoped that the inspector would not be timing everyone, so he selected the slowest person for each phase. The old and clumsy Uncle Yayli was one of workers assigned to assist the assessment process.

The day had come. Comrade Fekete, a small, unpretentious, nervous man with questionable hygiene and thick glasses on his nose, appeared at Ede's house on Trefort Street. You may remember his house had a large kitchen, where the Kádár's will work. They had a sewing machine that could be used for the assembly of the briefcases. Each phase of the production was represented and the people nervously waited for the arrival of the "man." He did not waste any time and took out a bunch of papers, pencils and the most important equipment: a large faced timer.

"Let the games begin." He attempted to make a joke, but it had no reaction from the nervous group. "Who will start?"

"I believe it is me," Uncle Yayli said with an anxious voice. He was wrong; first, the person who was stamping out the pieces had to start. It will be long day. Ede thought that he could convince this potentially corrupt bureaucrat to skip some steps in his calculation, so he could give them better rates.

This man wanted to spend one hour with each step for each product. He told everyone that he has to watch every move in order to come up with a truthful final calculation. After the stamping started, Ede asked Mr. Fekete to step out from the kitchen for a minute.

"I cannot leave him there. I need to watch everything he does."

"Please do not worry! He will continue without you, there is no way to cheat."

"Listen, I am sure you don't want to do this for days. Do you? I think we could do this in parallel. After 15 minutes, he will produce enough pieces for the next step."

"No, no, no short cuts!" the man contested. "I must do it as I originally described the method to my superiors. I do not want to get into any trouble. You must understand this, Mr. Kádár."

"Darn it," Ede was angry inside, and almost screamed out loud, but he whispered under his nose "this man happened to be a chicken, or an honest person. This is our luck." They went back to the kitchen, and the test continued. It took more than two whole days to complete the whole process, the inspector left for Budapest in the late morning of the third day. The waiting game has started. The waiting was nerve-racking, because not only the amount of money the group could earn was uncertain, but also the permission for the operation was hanging on a thin thread of hope all this was dependent on the findings of last three days. A few weeks passed before they received the results.

The results turned up to be much better than expected. Definitely using Uncle Yayli and the like for the "speed test" worked out. Soon after receiving the good news, Ede began to organize the workflow. He asked everyone to come to his house to discuss everyone's responsibility and the expected production schedule. Ede continued to be the manager of the whole operation, responsible for obtaining raw materials, organizing the shipping schedules and the most important job of paying off people (bribing) wherever it was deemed necessary. As the common fable would say, "wheels must be greased; otherwise the automobile will stop running." Ede was traveling to the leather factories in various cities to make sure they delivered on time. He personally visited Mr. Katz, not because he did not trust his friend Jenő, but Ede wanted to make sure that the payroll was calculated correctly by the accountant.

He visited the headquarters of the State Department Store in Budapest to talk to Dr. Gyula Kiss. This time, he was not there. Ede inquired about his whereabouts, but he got nowhere fast. What can he do? Without his help, the factory will be without a supporter. If the State Department Store would stop buying the products, the whole operation of the Remnants and Waste Recovery Company could be in jeopardy. In these times, personnel changes like this was not at all unusual, especially changing guards at high position job like this, but it was so "inconvenient." Corruption and political shakedowns were the rule of the day. Truly, it took serious efforts and careful manipulation to keep up with all changes. One had to be careful to ask because if you were considered a close ally of deposed leader, it could be the end of your career. It was useful and practical to know someone unimportant who may know something. These people were approachable without any possible danger. Ede aimlessly was walking on the beautiful, elegant Kossuth Lajos Street toward the river Danube. He noticed a man walking on the other side of the street. There were many people walking on the street this time of the day, but this man looked familiar to Ede. "I got it," Ede said half aloud, and people were looking at him as if he was crazy. He quickly crossed the wide avenue to catch up with Comrade Fekete. Ede recognized his nervous, unsure way of walking with his head down, as if he was afraid to see anyone.

"Good day, Mr. Fekete!" Ede greeted the surprised shy man.

"Oh, I know you from Békéscsaba, good day to you," he answered with a half-smile on his face. "What are you doing here?"

"I was looking for someone, but he is no longer working there. I need to find his replacement, but I do not know who to ask or where to go for help. Would you like to have a cup of coffee, if you are not busy, I need some company."

"Sure, I am on my break. I start working very early in the morning. I could use something to wake me up." Ede was surprised to see him being so friendly. He was guessing, since this conversation had nothing to do with work, their chitchat would be somewhat relaxing.

"The Emke coffeehouse is around the corner. Is this good for you?"

"Yes, occasionally I stop by for an espresso, but with my salary, I could not afford to be a steady guest." The two sat down in the exclusive, just recently renovated hotel lobby, which served as the coffeehouse. They were talking and Ede was waiting to pop the question about the new leadership at the Hungarian Working People's Party at the State department store, but he could not find the right moment. Eventually, Comrade Fekete started to talk about how happy he was to get a new job at the State Department Store. He was sure the new company would use his talent much better than his old one. "G-d is with me." Ede told himself.

"I knew some people there. I may know your boss." Ede came alive.

"I do not think you know my boss, Comrade Aradczky just moved here from Tatabanya. They wanted me to work with the party, but I felt I am more of a scientist than a politician." For a second he worryingly looked around, if anyone might have heard him.

"I am sure you will help the party regardless," Ede assured him.

"Comrade Lakatos, the Chairman, still thinks I should work for him, but he is not angry about my decision." Comrade Fekete was opening up to Ede. Ede did not even hear what he was saying after Ede had gotten the information he needed. Ede looked at his watch.

"I am sorry, I forgot the time. I must go it was good to see you again." He paid the waiter and rushed out to the street hoping the office of the State Department Store was still open. Ede took the elevator to the top floor, where the Chairman's office was and told the receptionist that he must speak to Chairman Lakatos about an urgent matter. To his surprise, he was escorted into the Chairman's office. Lakatos was older and more distinguished looking man than his predecessor was. Ede felt a bit easier in his company. Ede explained to Comrade Lakatos about the reemergence of the Remnants and Waste Recovery Company and asked for a continuance of the already existing business relationship. To his surprise, it was granted. Comrade

Lakatos thanked him for coming by, and promised the business relationship will be the same as it was in the past. Meaning, for the bribe, he will continue the relationship!

Ede was dizzy after he left the building. He could not believe what just happened and he was praying this was not a dream. It was getting to be late in the day and it was time for the evening prayer. He felt that he has to go to shul to thank G-d for today. He got home to Békéscsaba late in the night making Helen nervous and worried. She relaxed when Ede told her the events of the day. They both felt that again their future is looking a little bit brighter.

In later years, Ede and his workers made good money working from home. The word got out that the factory was doing well and more people wanted to join, but there was a limit to how many people the Remnants and Waste Recovery Company was allowed to employ. Making a decent living is the most important part of everybody's life. This was true for any era, but it was even more important for the Hungarians in this juncture of history. In the 1950's, life was made harder due to shortages of necessary goods and Communists interference with people's lives. Some extra eggs, another chicken, a nice pair of shoes, or a new dress made a world of difference for people.

15

Lacika is Laci now

In the meantime, Lacika was getting older. On September 1, 1954, Lacika entered the fourth grade; he was approaching his 11th birthday. On the first day of school, something strange happened when the homeroom teacher came into their classroom. There were four rows of desks in the classroom. The teacher told the boys on the left two rows to stand up, and in pairs, leave the classroom. The remaining kids were holding their breath while waiting what might happen next. A few minutes later, a bunch of crying girls appeared in the doorway and slowly sat down in the empty chairs. Everyone was in shock. The school was coed but, until now, boys and girls were attending separate classes. In Hungary, a class of students stayed together for all subjects. Throughout the day, different teachers were coming into the classrooms to teach them different subjects. The coed situation changed only one practice: gym classes were held separately.

It took some time until the boys and girls got used to being so close together. Some ignored the other gender, others, especially boys, were ready to make fools of themselves over pretty girls. Lacika also eyed a smiley faced, blond girl, Judi Biro. Lacika was shy and never revealed his affection towards this girl. Only in his dreams, he was a hero. A hero who saved his love from the evil king's solders, and killed them all. Unfortunately, at the end of his dream, before he could collect the reward, he always woke up and wondered what reward he would get from the girl for saving her. Gold, diamonds, rubies, no, a kiss, what he really wanted as a reward. It never happened. After school, Lacika would follow her to home, but making sure that the Judi would not see him. Occasionally, they were playing in the schoolyard that made him happy. For years, in his dreams she was his girlfriend, but during the day, it was a different story.

I mentioned the Rattai family and their daughter named Baba. She was attending the same class as Lacika. They got closer partly because they knew each other already, and their parents were friends. There was another attraction, she started to "develop," and Lacika was dying to steal a look at the budding chest of his friend. He tried to "accidently" touch it with more or less success. She was a tease; this young girl knew how to attract attentions from boys, any boy. This excitement kept their friendship alive for many years to come. Since in those days, talking about sex was a taboo, youngsters had to discover it by themselves. Some sooner, some later did experiment with the "forbidden fruit."

§ § § § § §

As we know already, Lacika really did not the drilling of the multiplication table, learning poems that made no sense or have any useful purpose, or memorizing historical dates like the birthdates of kings and dates of other historical events. Lacika wondered why it was so important to know the exact date, (day, month, and year) when Julius Cesar was born and died. Would not it been more useful and interesting to explain what he did to earn his fame?

After Lacika learned to read, he discovered how exiting a good book could be. He read many books written for young readers and later matured to reading serious classical books. A distant relative of the Kádár family, named Bella, had two unmarried daughters who were already at the age when people started to call them "old-maids. The older one was traveling and working somewhere, but no one was sure where and what she did. She had numerous relationships with man (married, not married, young, not so young). The other one, Olga, was much more subdued. She was a librarian working at the same library that Lacika frequently (once or twice a week) visited. Olga always helped Lacika in his reading selections, thus she molded his taste for books. Lacika would read a good book all night long if Helen did not make him go to sleep.

In the beginning, when Lacika learned to read, he liked fables and fairy tales from Hans Christian Andersen books, Fables of Benedek Apó written by Elek Benedek, a famous Hungarian writer, and others. Later, he started to read adventure stories like The Last of the Mohicans, Tom Sawyer, Robinson Crusoe, and Captain Nemo, a book that is better known as Twenty Thousand Leagues under the Sea written by the French writer Jules Verne, who was his favorite author forever. Soon, Lacika started reading books we call "Romantic Classical" from authors like Alexandre Dumas (The Three Musketeers and The Count of Monte Cristo), Victor Hugo (Les Misérables, also known as The Hunchback of Notre-Dame), also books written by Charles Dickens, Emile Zola, Honoré de Balzac, and Leo Tolstoy. He also enjoyed reading from one of the most famous Hungarian writer from the same era: Mór Jókai (A Man of Gold—Az Arany Ember, The Heartless Man's Sons—A Kőszívű Ember Fiai). In later years, Olga introduced him to some contemporary writers like Thomas Mann, Ernest Hemingway even Jean-Paul Sartre.

I could go on, but you get the idea. I have to apologize to my readers if I have listed authors that you may not know, but I needed to highlight his dedication (consciences or otherwise) to open his mind to everything useful and enjoyable. You must also know that reading was the best way to enhance your imagination. Reading the words that the author uses to describe a landscape, an article of clothing, a human feeling of love, a despicable event would paint that image in your mind. Going to a movie or a play, you will see only the way the director and the actor interprets the same images that most likely will be different from yours. Many times, I heard the saying, "I will read it when it becomes a movie." People thinking this way will lose their ability to dream.

Lacika was a shy child. He never had many friends. Who would be friendly with a kid whose life was controlled by strange rules? He could not go to play with other kids after sundown on Friday until Saturday night. He could not eat anything at anyone's house, because he was allowed to eat kosher food only. His best friend, maybe the only good friend, was Sanyi Mészáros, who was sitting next to him throughout elementary school. Sanyi did not care about Lacika's restrictions. The two kids were playing nicely together at either Lacika's house or Sanyi's house. Sanyi's parents understood never question Lacika's restrictions. The two went for long bicycle rides or played chess in the winter. The two never had any fights for all the years they were friends.

Talking about fights, unfortunately, Lacika had a few. As I mentioned before, anti-Semitism is a product of ignorance and a lack of proper education. In the elementary school, Lacika was exposed all kinds of children. Children were coming from well-educated families and children were coming from broken homes. One of the kids, named Vince, was coming from latter group. He was always in trouble in school; he always found a way to get into mischief or many times into serious trouble. Instead of concentrating on studying, he was looking for a way to look "cool" to his peers. By the way, he was a few years older than Lacika but was still attending fourth grade. You must remember that the idea of "social promotion" was not invented yet and kids who were not able to pass minimum grade requirements were held back. I still remember a kid about 16 years old still attending six grades in my school.

Getting back to Vince, he started to pick on Lacika.

"Hey kids, do you see this, part of his penis was cut off." He was referring to the circumcision of Jewish kids. In Hungary, only Jewish boys were circumcised. The kids were surrounding Lacika and they demanded:

"Show us your dick!"

"NO," screamed Lacika and tried to break away. The kids were grabbing him to try to take his pants off. Adults were walking by and did nothing. Finally, he got away and with tears in his eyes, he was running home. He was afraid to say anything when he got home.

These kinds of problems were relatively frequent and Vince was always in the middle. If Lacika saw this bully, he would try to sneak by him or go the other way whenever he was around. These incidents started to be more violent and Lacika could no longer shield them away from Ede. Ede went to the principal to complain, but got nowhere. When Vince found out about Ede complaining to the principal, he and his buddies went after Lacika. The police did not help much. They went to Vince's mother, but she told them that she is working all day. Vince is roaming around without any supervision. She cannot control her child. What else could she do?

Ede had to do something. He got an idea.

"Lacika, I need to talk to you." Lacika got scared, maybe he did something wrong and carefully went to his father.

"Do you remember when I was telling you many stories? You may remember this one: Fülöp, I cannot remember his last name." Ede started his story with his usual excited voice.

"That is OK; I will forget his name anyway." Lacika was encouraging his father.

"He was a well to do merchant not living among the "Ghetto," where most Jews were living in Budapest. It was in the thirties, when the stupid Hungarian youth tried to imitate the activities of the Hitler-Yugend in Germany. They constantly molested him while he was walking home to his beautiful apartment on the banks of the Danube. They were envious of

his possessions, his wealth, and his social standing. Unfortunately, he was not one of those people who could stand up for himself. You know, these despicable people can sense weakness. It is easy to pick on the weak. My friend, Pista Greewald, was a big man; he was about 185 centimeter tall and about 90 kilos. He belonged to the MTK boxing club, which consisted of primarily Jewish athletes. He heard about poor Fülöp and his problems. So what did Pista do? He convinced some of his friends at the club to take care of this problem. He talked to Fülöp and told him to be brave and confront those guys on the next day."

"This is what happened: When these guys came, Fülöp get all his strength together and looked them into the eyes and with a somewhat shaky voice he screamed at them. "You people shame on you! Why are you bothering me? Go away!"

"So what will you do, you stinking Jew?"

"I will beat the hell out of you!" This comment triggered genuine laughter from the group. They were laughing so hard that they had hard time talking.

"Will you do you this by yourself or will some of your miserable weakling friends help you? They were even more amused when two similar built Jewish kids appeared in the back. "You must be kidding? We will eat them alive," said the leader and they started to approach Fülöp with harmful intentions.

"Hey," yelled Pista, "are you sure you want to do this?" He and five of his buddies surrounded the gang. They had no chance; the living daylight was beaten out of the gang. They have never gone close to Fülöp again."

"Are these people still around?" Lacika was asking anxiously.

"Some died in the concentration camps and others are far away from here, besides they are too old to fight"

"So how this story will help me?"

"Well let me explain. You must be brave like Fülöp, but unfortunately you have to take care of this by yourself."

"I cannot, there are too many of them."

"That is Ok. You are wearing this heavy, strong Ski boot with metal protecting the front of the sole of the shoe. If you would kick someone with it hard, it would hurt!"

"Kick someone where?"

"Well, you must know that a man has two vulnerable areas in his body: his shin and between his legs." As I told you Lacika was bashful, withdrawn. He was by no means athletic, wearing thick glasses; he was an ideal candidate as a target for bullies even if he were not Jewish. Today's term we would call him a geek, but this term was not invented yet in those days.

One beautiful unusually sunny winter day, Lacika was cutting through the small park behind the school on his way home. From nowhere the "gang" appeared front of him and the five boys started to push him around. The ground was frozen and slippery, so he fell and almost started to cry. Then he remembered his father. He got up, swept off the snow from his pants, turned around, and said:

"Please do not do this." His heart was throbbing in his throat from the excitement and fear of consequences. They stopped for a second and broke up laughing (like in the story that his father told him), so he bravely continued with more steady voice:

"Stop this, or else!"

"Did any one hear something?" Vince said laughing with a somewhat surprised tone in his voice. "What did you say?"

"I said, get out of here, and leave me alone." His speech was followed by more amusement. They decided it was enough and they came closer to Lacika. Then something big happened and surprised everyone present.

Lacika gathered all his strength, all his courage and stepped closer to one of the smaller kids and his right feet swung making a cracking noise after finding its target the boy's shin. Lacika did not wait for the result: he ran home as fast as he could and kept repeating to himself all the way home. "I did it! I did it. I did it?"

"What happened?" Helen asked. "Why are you so red? Did anyone hurt you again? Talk to me."

"Is daddy home? I need to talk to him."

"Yes, he is home in the bedroom." Lacika ran to the bedroom without stopping.

"Daddy I have done it! I did it!"

"Ok, slow down. What did you do?"

"What did I do? I have done what you told me to do!"

"I have told you a lot of things. What specifically I had told you to do?"

"You told me about Fülöp, do you remember?" The disappointed Lacika was in the verge of crying.

"No, I do not recall him. Please tell me what did you do that has made you so exited?" Lacika told his story, but at this stage, he was not sure if his father was appreciating his accomplishment. Ede was truly surprised about what happened, but he was concerned of the consequences of his son's action. On the other hand, he was happy, because his son finally stood up for himself. Ede explained to Lacika about his worry about what would happen next.

"Lacika you must know that violence is not always the answer to solve everything. The youngster ended up in the hospital with his shin broken. I am sure his parents are sad."

"But Daddy you told me a story where your friends taught a lesson to people treating us Jews badly."

"Yes now I remember, but you must understand those were different times."

"Is there any good time to treat us like dirt?"

"Lacika, you are right. Nobody ever should treat us without respect. Let us hope that the parents will never tell it to the police. On the other hand, I am truly proud of the fact that you stood up for yourself." Around the town, the word got out and decent people were quietly happy. Others may have gotten the "message," and this incident has established some kind of "respect' for Lacika. Lacika was not 100% sure, but he believed that his action has contributed to the fewer number anti-Semitic incidences he encountered in the next few years. A few weeks passed and Lacika approached his father and gingerly asked him.

"Daddy, may I ask you a question?"

"Sure, what is it?"

"I think the name Lacika is very childish. After that incident, I am not a child anymore."

"Really?" Ede was amused. "Why is that, you are still only 11 years old."

"I know that, but I feel I need more respect than a name of "Lacika" would give me."

"As a Jew you will be considered an adult when you become 13 years old."

"I know that." Lacika stopped for a moment before continuing, took deep breath and another. "I would like everyone to call me Laci, it is still a nickname, but it sounds more respectable."

"If this MAN wants to be called Laci it is fine with me. But, you may want to be called with your full name Laszlo, which would be even more respectful."

"No, no, no, Laci is fine, thank you." Laci ran into the house and proudly announced to his mother "Daddy has decided to call me Laci from now on." Hearing this, Helen was fighting off laughter and her face developed a funny looking expression.

"Where is this coming from?" she asked Ede, who just walked into the house.

"Well, your son wants to be treated as a "mature boy," so we need to treat him with more respect." Ede also tried not to laugh and continued with a deep voice: "My son's name from this day shall be LACI." Helen could not stop the urge to giggle anymore and busted out laughing. Laci was confused and he was hurt.

"Why is this so funny?"

"Sorry," Helen said, "but my dear Laci, without the "ka" is not you. "You do not become more respectable because you're being called with a different name, you gain respect with the way you behave."

"I still do not understand why this is so funny."

"Listen, it may not be so funny, but we called you Lacika forever and to me Laci is not you, to me he is somebody else."

"But it is still me!" Lacika was losing his temper.

"Listen, we will call you Laci from now on, is this right Daddy?"

"It is settled, Laci." Ede gave his blessing for the "name change," after all, by this time he has passed his tenth birthday.

16

the year 1956

The year was 1956, a year with great significance and consequence in the history of Communist Hungary.

Numerous international events were influencing the Hungarian political scene. Stalin's death in 1953 created a vacuum in the Soviet leadership. A new party leader, Nikita Khrushchev, victoriously emerged after years of struggle to gain full power against the old Stalinist allies. In February 1956, Khrushchev in his "secret speech" denounced Stalin and his protégés, promising a "less repressive era" and starting a period of liberalization. This "secret speech" was slowly disclosed and its contents spread to the satellite countries like Poland, Czechoslovakia, Romania, and Hungary providing hope for more political freedom.

In 1955, Austria re-established itself as a free independent and democratic state. Furthermore, Austria declared itself a permanent politically neutral state. As the result of the treaty, the Allies left all Austrian territories on October 25, 1955.

The leaders in the top of the ruling elite were unhappy; the person who was extremely unhappy was Mátyás Rákosi, who did not like to be "second fiddle" to the Prime Minister Imre Nagy. Rákosi did everything in his power to undermine most of the reforms implemented by Nagy and these actions of Rákosi discredited Nagy and removed as Prime Minister. On July 18, 1956, Rákosi was replaced by Ernő Gerő as the General Secretary of the Party. This was triggered by Khrushchev's determination to get rid of all Stalin-era leaders.

In June 1956, the violent uprising of Polish workers was brutally put down by the Polish government. A more moderate reformist, Władysław Gomułka, was appointed as First Secretary of the Polish

Worker's Party. He was able to negotiate concessions, Soviet troop reductions, and other trade related reforms from Moscow.

USA policies toward Hungary and other Eastern Bloc countries were changed to encourage them to try to break away from the control of the Soviet Union.

The resignation of Mátyás Rákosi set off a feeling that a new era was on the horizon. Students, writers, and journalists started to get involve with politics and organized forums to discuss the problems in Hungary. The university students in Szeged established a democratic student organization and within a week, more of these organizations formed throughout the country. On October 22, the students compiled a list of "Sixteen Points" containing several national policy demands. On the afternoon of October 23, about 20,000 people gathered at a statue of a war hero of the 1848 revolution, where they read the manifesto and chanted patriotic songs. Someone in the crowd cut out the communist coat-of-arms from the Hungarian flag, and others quickly followed suit. Later, the crowd crossed the Danube to join demonstrators outside the Parliament Building. By 6 p.m., the peaceful crowd grew to more than 200,000 people. Ernő Gerő broadcasted a speech denouncing the demands. The crowd, angered by the hard rejections, decided to take matters into their own hands and toppled Stalin's statue. The crowd celebrated by placing Hungarian flags with the Communist coat-of-arms cut out into Stalin's boots, which was all that was left of the statue.

At the same time, a large crowd gathered by the radio building and demanded they be allowed to read the manifesto over the air. First, tear gas was tossed into the crowd of people, later the Secret Service (AVH) opened fire killing and wounding many. Soldiers were sent to help the AVH, but many sided with the people. That night, 23 Soviet tanks entered Budapest requested by Ernő Gerő. Soviet tanks were positioned in key points of the city, in the meantime, the armed revolutionaries set up barricades to defend the city. Imre Nagy became prime minister and called for an end of to the violence, but the population started to arm itself and some sympathetic Soviet troops refused to shoot at people.

On October 25, a massive protest in front of the Parliament Building invoked fire from AVH and the crowd shot back. The government collapsed forcing Ernő Gerő to flee to the Soviet Union and left Imre Nagy as the Prime Minister and János Kádár the First secretary of the Communist Party. The fighting continued until a ceasefire was arranged on Oct 28 and by October 30, most Soviet troops left Budapest. The country felt invigorated, most political prisoners were released, and the AVH was abolished and a multi-party system was proposed.

§ § § § § §

The new school year started promptly on September 1, 1956. Laci (remember, no more Lacika) started the fifth grade. Russian, a new subject, was included into his curriculum. The well-educated Hungarians would learn one of two foreign languages in their lifetime, since the Hungarian language is like no other language in the world. Hungarian was a useful language in Hungary, but nowhere else in the world. The Magyars traced their origins somewhere deep into Asia. The forefathers had been swept into the westward migrations of Asians and many centuries passed before they finally reached present day Hungary. Here, they were wedged between the ever-westward migrating Asians and the more established Western European nations. The language the Magyars (Hungarians) brought with them had virtually no relationship to any other European languages. Research proved that in present day Europe, the Finnish and Estonian languages were loosely related to the Hungarian language, but the many centuries of separation wiped out most language similarities.

The choice of a second language for most Hungarians was German. For many centuries, the Habsburgs were controlling most of Hungary and in general, the Germanic influence was apparent throughout Central European history. Now that the Russians were in control of Central Europe, they too wanted to spread their own Russian culture. The Russian language is not an easy language to learn. After a few days of study, Laci was joking about all the "blisters" on his tongue caused by the hard pronunciation of Russian words. The truth was nobody wanted to study the Russian language, but the schoolchildren had no choice in this manner.

The school year had hardly started when one day there was good news, at least for the students. The teachers announced that today the schools will be closed and it may be closed tomorrow, no further explanations were given. Most children do not like going to school, so there was a general euphoria among the kids. It was October 23, 1956. Laci heard adults talking about riots, revolution, counterrevolution, but he did not understand what was going on besides he was happy to miss school. A few days later, the school was reopened to the overwhelming disapproval of the kids. A new homeroom-teacher came in to the class and announced that the teaching will continue, but some changes will be instituted. The forced learning of the Russian language would be stopped and if any students wanted to study German or English, they were welcome to enroll.

Some of the parents were cautious; others were ready to allow their child to enroll in English or German classes. People were whispering among themselves about big changes on the horizon. Most of the news came from the Radio Free Europe or the Voice of America. Until now, these radio stations had been forbidden to listen to, but most everyone was listening anyway even though they were risking some consequences of harsh punishment. Most citizens did not believe the news from the official newscast that was controlled and censored by the central Communist Government.

Laci was amazed how fast people were spreading the news during the first two days of the uprising that would later be name the "Counterrevolution."

"The Russians are leaving Budapest and they will soon leave Hungary."

"A new cabinet has formed in Budapest, we will all be free."

"The Americans will help us to free ourselves from the Soviets."

"Some anti-Semites started to kill us Jews in Budapest."

"I heard otherwise, they got killed because these Jews were in the AVH, not because they were Jews."

"In Budapest there is an all-out war between the everyday people and the Russians. The people are winning!"

"A Soviet soldier was shot in Békéscsaba; the Russian will kill us all!"

"Did you hear? Comrade Nyiri talked to the Soviet commander and he convinced him not to take any revenge on the people of Békéscsaba. He speaks perfect Russian."

"He is my Russian language teacher," Laci injected. "I do not like him. He did not like me, because I am Jewish"

"Nyiri became the head of Local Revolutionary Council of the city. The people have elected him as appreciation for saving the city."

"I hope they will not be coming for us Jews again."

"I hope the Russians will stay to protect us Jews."

Indisputably, many people were in panic including Jews. They were afraid of the consequences of the uprising whether or not they were involved in the riots. Soviets most likely would win against the rioters and as history has proven, the victors would rule in terror. Instantaneously, Jews in Békéscsaba organized trucks to flee to Austria, the closest non-Soviet controlled country. Word came that the borders were opening up and both Jews and non-Jews were fleeing. Everyday people were trying to escape from Hungary as soon as possible because most people were pessimistic in believing things will change for the better; the Russians will come back, they would not allow anyone, any country to escape from their grip.

Helen and Ede were afraid to leave for an unknown, questionable destination. The fragile health of Helen held the family back from the potentially dangerous journey crossing the Hungarian-Austrian border, the "Iron-Curtain." More than 200,000 Hungarians made it to freedom during these unstable times of the Hungarian Revolution in 1956.

For a few days, life returned to being somewhat normal in Békéscsaba. Children were attending school people returned to their workplaces, stores were opened for business. Békéscsaba was too far from Budapest to be affected by the events of the capitol city.

§ § § § § §

"Laci, Laci wake up!"

"Whaaat?"

"You must get up right now!" screamed Ede, but Laci was having a hard time waking up. It was pitch black outside.

"What time is it? Why do I need to get up now?" Laci tried to assess the situation. Then, he heard a loud whistling sound and the streets were lit up like sunshine in the middle of the night.

"It is four o'clock in the morning," Ede replied with a scared face, because another piercing sound crushed the usual peaceful night of the city where normally only the voices of barking dogs were heard.

"Are these fireworks?" Laci, with a happy face, was asking his father.

"God sake no, the Russians are firing at the city. We must get out of here." Helen was dressed and gave Laci a warm outfit. Several packages were put together and the family was ready to flee. Laci was taking his own pillow and a blanket. Helen and Ede were taking food and other valuables and they quietly left the house.

This was a special day in Hungarian history. It was November 4, 1956. This was the day when the mighty Soviet Army moved back in and started to crush the revolution.

"Where are we going? Why are we leaving our house?" Laci was asking questions for which he was not given any answers. It was cold and scary outside. The "lightning" and "thundering" was constant. The streets were empty, not a soul on the streets, only the Kádár family was abandoning their comfortable shelter. One of the missiles came down close to them with a loud noise and hit the ground nearby. That was very scary. Laci remembered the story of Sodom and Gomorrah from the bible where G-d was destroying the cities by brimstone and fire. He was afraid to look back avoiding the fate of Lot's wife who turned into a pillar of salt.

They arrived at the Rattai family's house. The family was up. They were not able to sleep from the thunderous outside noises.

"Can we stay by you?" Ede asked when Mrs. Rattai let the Kádár family in. "We are afraid to stay in our big house, because I have seen in the past that the Russians would take the biggest, nicest house for their headquarters and I do not want to be there when it happens."

"No problem Mr. Kádár, we have a spare room you and your wife could stay there until you need to and Lacika could stay with my kids."

The adults were talking and Laci was bunked down on the floor with his pillow and blanket. The kids were wide-awake and they were having fun, forgetting about all the scary noises around them. It was about 6:00 am by the time the shooting stopped and it became quiet, the "war" was over and the kids finally could fall asleep.

Everyone slept late. Laci woke up first in the kid's room and for a minute, he thought he was still asleep seeing the unfamiliar surroundings. Then he remembered last night's events. He was wondering what they would do next. He moved around quietly in the room, Baba and Jancsi were resting in their own bed deeply asleep. The room was pleasantly warm and Baba must have been hot, because her blanket was completely down on the floor and she was on her back covered by only her nightshirt.

Until now, Laci had never noticed that she was "well developed" for her age of 12. To the great excitement of Laci, her nightgown was soft and it revealed her already curvaceous body. Laci held his breath and he silently inched closer to her bed. He bent over her and to Laci's amazement, her budding breasts were partially revealed. He had never seen one in the "flesh" before. He was fixated on this wonderful sight for a while forgetting the time. He looked at the girl's face and to his horror, he saw her wide-open blue eyes, "I have never noticed that she has beautiful blue eyes before," told himself. Her face was all smiles with a playful twinkle in the corner of her eye, and then with a fast move she covered herself. Lacika was so embarrassed. He was not sure that his embarrassment was coming from the experience or from the fact that he was discovered. He became red from head to toe and run out from the room.

In the kitchen, breakfast was served and everyone sat down to eat. The adults were discussing the events and were listening to the radio. Earlier on the radio, they heard the last speech of Imre Nagy. He was broadcasting his final plea to the nation and to the world for help, announcing that Soviet Forces were attacking Budapest. His speech was interrupted when the Soviet troops occupied the Parliament building. Gunfights were reported in and around Budapest between the attacking Russians and some Hungarian Army units along with freedom fighters. The Soviet tanks were indiscriminately firing at civilian and military targets causing heavy casualties to people and buildings. The fighting lasted for two days and since no outside help from western countries came, the revolution was defeated.

§ § § § § §

The parents were afraid to let the children out, so they were playing inside the house. They did not bother to change into street clothes and they remained in their nightgowns. Baba enjoyed being flirtatious, especially towards the naïve, inexperienced Laci. For a short time, Laci would not look at Baba because he was still embraced. Baba understood what was going on in Laci's mind, and she decided to flirt with him for the rest of the day. Every time she bent down to pick up something from the floor, she made sure that her top become visible to Laci. How could he not notice the full view of her budding breasts? His eyes were as a magnet fixated on the "mountains and valleys" of his friend. This went on for days. What could a 12 years old boy, with his hormones acting like a "man," do in a situation like this? Naturally, Laci was hoping and wishing he would never have to leave their house. He wanted to continue and hoped "something" would happen between him and Baba... but what? He was not sure, but certainly wanted to touch them! Part of his wish came through, Ede decided it was still dangerous to go out and they would stay here for at least one more night.

Laci could not sleep from his excitement. He kept looking into Baba's bed and tried to get yet another glimpse of those exiting things. Even when he was thinking of them, he felt something in his groin area that felt good. Well, he had no luck, the room was cold and she was all bundled up, there was no chance for any voyeurism tonight.

On the next day around noon, Ede decided to look around outside. It was Friday and they needed to prepare food for Sabbath. Ede came back with lots of news. The Russians did not take over his house and the Kádár family could go safely home. Nyiri was arrested along with many so-called "anti-revolutionaries." Soviet tanks were patrolling the streets, but they did not bother anyone so far. Everything was closed and a curfew was announced for after eight in the evening.

"Could I stay more?" Laci was hoping for more excitement, but to his disappointment, he was ordered to go home.

"May I come to visit you soon?" he asked Baba.

"You know that you are welcome anytime." Baba was teasing Laci by touching her top and had a wide smile on her cute face.

"Daddy, when can I come back?"

"What is going on?' Ede was wondering, as a "ladies" man he noticed the flirtation and with a smiling face he continued, "You hardly ever came to play with Baba before. Now, I am thinking, you did not come here since school was started."

"I know," Baba said, "I think Laci does not like me since we became classmates."

"It is not true, I always liked you, but at the school it is different, and I need to have boys as my friend not girls."

"That is not true I know you are eying Judi." Both Helen and Ede was amazed about this "jealous" conversation between the two kids. As far as they knew, Laci was very shy especially with girls.

"No time to waste, we have to get home to prepare for Shabbat." Helen nudged Laci to go. For the first time in many years, Ede and Laci did not go to shul Friday night and Saturday morning, but Laci had to say all the Friday night prayers. He had to say even more than usual, because Ede made him say other prayers to thank G-d they came home safely and to ask him for further protection.

Slowly, life returned to normal, if you can consider having Soviet soldiers patrolling the streets, guarding all the government buildings and with no Hungarian police being seen anywhere as normal. School was reopened again and people went to work. Everyone tried to ignore the ever-visible Soviet military presence.

§ § § § § §

By October 31, 1956, most of the Soviet army units stationed in Hungary left, but a new set of military personnel was moved back on or about November 4, 1956 to crush the revolution. These solders were from the Far East and judging by their faces and their heights they were from Mongolia. Looking at their faces, they looked like uneducated, fearless fighters. Besides a rifle, they were also carrying a long bayonet attached to their belt. Laci had never seen such a frightening looking people. Even the Russian soldiers he had seen before did not give these "wild animal" like impressions. Every time Laci, the big boy, was walking by places these soldiers were standing as guards, he crossed the street; these soldiers were a frightening sight for a 12 year old.

Life for Laci returned to normal. He was attending school, where changes were introduced again. Before the 1956 revolution, children were forced to become members of the Hungarian Pioneer Movement (Magyar Úttörők Szövetsége.) The purpose for this young communist organization was to educate youngsters to become the future generation's communists. Now, school age children had to reapply for their membership and others could opt out. Laci never again had to be a pioneer. The learning of the Russian language became mandatory again. Some teachers lost their jobs and others took their place.

For many years to come Ede continued working for the Remnants and Waste Recovery Company and was able to provide a comfortable life for his family.

Epilogue

Budapest was fully under Soviet control by November 8, 1956. János Kádár became Prime Minister of the new Government and General Secretary of the Hungarian Communist Party. Few Hungarians rejoined the reorganized Party "Hungarian Socialist Workers Party (MSZMP)," its old leadership was purged. Kádár steadily increased his control over Hungary and neutralized dissenters. After 1956, the Soviet Union severely purged the Hungarian Army and reinstituted political indoctrination in the units that remained. In May 1957, the Soviet Union increased its troop levels in Hungary and Hungary accepted the Soviet presence on a permanent basis. Thousands of Hungarians were arrested and were brought before the Hungarian courts, sentenced, and imprisoned, and several hundred were executed.

The Jewish population of Békéscsaba was reduced to a fraction of the 500 or so Jews who came back after the Holocaust. All ultra religious Jews left, including the Rabbi Schnitzler, Mr. Neiman, the religion teacher, dear uncle Yayli, and many more. Most orthodox kids also disappeared with their parents from Békéscsaba after 1956, leaving Laci the only youngster who kept Jewish laws in the entire Jewish community of Békéscsaba and the surrounding area.

The community was left without a Rabbi, a shochet, Chazan (Cantor), and Shamash so the community had a hard time keeping daily minyan (quorum of ten), and in later years even for Friday night and Saturday it was difficult to get the required 10 people together for prayers.

The Jewish community had to reorganize itself. The community became a community of old people. Hardly any children and people under 40 years of age remained. A new president was elected, one of the few remaining orthodox men, Mr. Berkowits affirmed himself as the Rabbi and shochet. Out of the remaining Jews, he was best qualified for this job, and he was able to keep this position for many years to come. To be able to keep Shabbat, he was earning his living as a traveling flea-market vendor selling various clothing items.

Over the years, members of the Jewish community of Békéscsaba slowly disappeared. Many Jewish people either immigrated to Israel or moved to Budapest to join a larger Jewish community. The elderly and sick from the effects of the concentration camps slowly passed away. By the mid 1960's, hardly any Jews stayed behind and those who did, had little or no affiliation with Jewish life, with Jewish identity, with the synagogue. Ede and Helen remained in Békéscsaba accepting yet another setback. Keeping a Kosher home became harder than ever before.

Laci left to attend a University in Szeged and he never returned to Békéscsaba. The Kádár family was finally able to immigrate to the USA in 1966.

Made in the USA
Lexington, KY
07 August 2013